Frank R. Stockton

FRANK R. STOCKTON

FRANK R. STOCKTON

A Critical Biography

By

MARTIN I. J. GRIFFIN

KENNIKAT PRESS, INC./PORT WASHINGTON, N. Y.

FRANK R. STOCKTON

Copyright 1939 by University of Pennsylvania Press
Reissued in 1965 by Kennikat Press by arrangement

Library of Congress Catalog Card No: 65-18606

Manufactured in U. S. A. by Arno Press, Inc.

Preface

No adequate biography of Frank R. Stockton exists. It is to be questioned whether an "adequate" biography of any man exists, but the universal human interest in other men's lives makes valuable even a poor attempt to tell what one man did—how he lived, how he looked, what ideas he expressed, how much his work contributed to the world, how much his worth contributed to human dignity. This critical biography of Frank R. Stockton attempts to piece together details of his life, many of which have not before been integrated into a complete chronological sequence, and, in so doing, to illustrate how much of Stockton's life was represented in his work. A second, but not secondary purpose, is to place Stockton and his work in proper perspective in the history of American literature.

Selective bibliographies, and short histories of American literature which mention Stockton at all, choose from the considerable body of his work a few stories as representative, and dismiss him as if those few were the only stories of permanent interest which he had written. It is true that "The Lady, or the Tiger?", *Rudder Grange,* and *The Casting Away of Mrs. Lecks and Mrs. Aleshine* are among Stockton's best work, but these are by no means all of Stockton's finer stories, and they alone should not be used as the measure of his achievement. His real achievement will, I hope, be clear from the pages which follow, compiled, in so far as possible, from original sources, and from the memories of those who knew Stockton.

After Stockton's death in 1902, Mrs. Stockton sold their home, Claymont, near Charles Town, West Virginia, and moved to Georgetown, in the District of Columbia. Here she remained until her death in 1906, when it was discovered that a great part of the documentary material in her possession—letters, diaries, journals, daybooks, scrapbooks, manuscripts—had been accidentally burned or purposely destroyed. What remained was divided among the nephews and nieces of Stockton by the terms of his will. In the course of twenty-five years much of the remaining material was lost or scattered. It is this fact which has prevented a wider knowledge of many of the details of Stockton's life. This present work does not attempt to remedy the irremedial but, through the kindness of many, it essays to present a completer picture of Stockton than has hitherto been available.

Mrs. George E. Cantrell, of Haddonfield, New Jersey, Stockton's niece, has been most generous in lending me valuable letters, scrapbooks, and the several Stockton manuscripts in her possession. In addition, her alert memory has solved many of my problems. I am indebted also to another of Stockton's nieces, the late Mrs. William A. McAllister, of Westfield, New Jersey, and to her husband, Mr. William A. McAllister, for their patient helpfulness under successive barrages of questions, extending over a period of several years. Not the least aid they have given me has been their consistent sympathy and encouragement.

I am indebted also for various items to the following: to the late William F. Clarke, of Scarsdale, New York, Stockton's successor on *St. Nicholas Magazine,* and later its editor, for personal anecdotes and factual material; to Mrs. Henry L. Wilson, of Columbus, Ohio, for notes which her husband, the late Henry L. Wilson, of Temple University, had made before his tragic death by automobile, on a journey in pursuit of Stockton material; to Dr. Robert J. Hunter, of the Philadelphia General Hospital, for permission to study the records of the hospital for the years of William Stockton's stewardship; to Dr. Joseph S. Hepburn, of Hahnemann Medical School, Historian of the Central High School, Philadelphia, for information on the early history of the school, and Stockton's years as a student there; to Mrs. J. M. Dodge, and her

PREFACE

son, Mr. Kern Dodge, of Philadelphia, for the valuable letters written by Stockton to Mary Mapes Dodge; to Mr. Walter L. Pforzheimer, of New York, for encouragement; to Mr. V. Valta Parma, of the Library of Congress, for valuable bibliographical assistance. My mother, Mrs. Wm. L. J. Griffin has spent long hours in libraries copying tedious pages of material from which I have extracted many facts concerning Stockton's antecedents.

My thanks are due to Charles Scribner's Sons, D. Appleton-Century Co., Harper and Brothers, and Dodd, Mead and Co., for permission to quote from stories to which they hold the copyrights.

I owe an especial debt of gratitude to Professor William L. Werner, of Pennsylvania State College, whose aid has been invaluable, and whose interest has made him long-suffering. His study of Stockton, "The Escapes of Frank Stockton," has many times been helpful, and he has most generously given me free use of his own laboriously collected material on Stockton.

Two other debts I owe. One, to my wife, whose faith has been as constant as her name; the other, to Dr. Arthur Hobson Quinn, of the University of Pennsylvania, a great teacher who has inspired one of his lesser students with some of his own zeal for truth and beauty, and whose help on many occasions and in many ways I shall never be able adequately to acknowledge.

M.I.J.G.

January 15, 1939

Contents

Frank R. Stockton

Chapter I

WHEN Francis Richard Stockton was born on April 5, 1834, the Stockton family had been established in New Jersey for nearly two hundred years. Richard Stockton, the founder of the American branch of the family, came to America sometime before 1656, settling first in Flushing, Long Island, but later moving permanently to Oneanickon, Burlington County, West Jersey.[1]

Richard Stockton, an industrious farmer, was the son of John Stockton of Malpas Parish, County Chester, England, whose lineage was traced through a female heir to David de Stockton. Records of David de Stockton's accession to the Manor of Stockton in the year 1250 are extant. Richard Stockton was of well-to-do yeomen stock, and brought with him from England sufficient money to establish himself securely on good farmland, in a country predominantly agricultural. He died in 1707, but a son by a second marriage, John (1674–1745), passed on the Stockton line through his son Daniel (1705–1763).

By 1730 the third generation of Stocktons was well established in Burlington County. Many of the English customs in which Richard had been trained persisted in the family, one of which was a system of primogeniture, modified by American influences. Stockton males married young, bought farms of their own nearby in Burlington County, or in other northern New Jersey counties, and reared large families. Daniel Stockton

[1] Details of the Stockton genealogy have been taken from a genealogical history of the Stockton family in the possession of Mrs. George E. Cantrell, of Haddonfield, N.J.

married Hanna Fisher, also of Burlington County, in 1728. She gave birth to eleven children. The second child of this marriage, John (1730–1763), married Hannah Jones, of Burlington County, in 1750, well in the by-now established tradition of the Stockton family to marry young and rear a family near the original Stockton homestead. Perhaps some of the Scotch ancestry of the Stocktons accounted for this apparent clannishness, but whatever its source, it remained a characteristic of the family until it was broken by the lack of a male heir in the nineteenth century.

The sixth and last child from the marriage of John Stockton to Hannah Jones was Samuel (1762–1847) the sturdy, octogenarian grandfather of Francis Richard Stockton. In 1784, Samuel Stockton married Hannah Gardiner, of Burlington, N.J.[2] By this first marriage of Samuel Stockton there were nine children.[3]

William Smith Stockton (1785–1860) was the first son, born April 8, 1785. The influence of a sternly Methodist household early formed him in a pattern from which he never deviated. Wesleyan theology and Methodist practice were the absorbing topics of which he never wearied. In 1807, on his twenty-second birthday, he married Elizabeth Sophia Hewlings, of Rutherford. In 1808 was born the first of the six children [4] of this marriage, Thomas Hewlings Stockton, Methodist minister, Chaplain to Congress. William Stockton's first wife contracted tuberculosis about the time of the birth of her last child, Elizabeth, in 1817. The disease progressed slowly but on August 10, 1826, she died. Two years later, in 1828, William Stockton married Emily Hepsibeth Drean [5] of

[2] It is an interesting coincidence that grandfather (Daniel), father (John), and son (Samuel), should all have married women of the same name, Hannah, from the same county, Burlington.

[3] After his wife's death in 1817, Samuel married a second time. The second marriage was to Vashti Austin, the widow of his brother-in-law, John Gardiner. There were no children.

[4] Thomas Hewlings, 1808; Emily Louise, 1810; Hannah, 1812; Samuel, 1813; Francis Asbury, 1815; Elizabeth Hewlings, 1817.

[5] Emily Drean was the daughter of John Drean of Belfast, Ireland, later of Leesburg, Virginia. He served under Lafayette in the Revolution, and was present at Cornwallis' surrender at Yorktown.

Leesburg, Virginia. By this second marriage there were nine children, the first two of whom died in infancy.[6]

Francis Richard, the third child of this second marriage, was thus the eldest son, and according to the English tradition to which all the Stockton's had adhered, he became, upon the death of his father, the leader of the younger family, as Thomas Hewlings was the leader of the older.

The Stocktons have had, therefore, a long history in America. They were of English yeoman stock, sturdy Methodist churchmen. They were good citizens, good neighbors, godly men. Of them all, none was more concerned with religion than William Smith Stockton. Of scant formal education, he was well read in the Bible and the exegetical classics of Wesleyanism. In 1820 he published his first book,[7] which set the temper and the tempo of the stream of pamphlets and articles which he wrote during his long life. For a time after his marriage, William Stockton served as clerk in the store of his uncle (by marriage), David Fenton, a leading publisher of Trenton. In 1827 he moved to Philadelphia, to join the staff of the Philadelphia Almshouse, as Agent.

In 1827 the Philadelphia Almshouse, founded in 1728, functioned also as a hospital, its original purposes having been altered by changing times. The bald term "almshouse," therefore, has an unfortunate connotation. When William Stockton joined the hospital staff in 1827, the necessity for larger quarters than those available at Tenth and Spruce Streets had become so pressing that plans were already under way for the construction of new buildings outside the city. Stockton was appointed house agent, an important executive position then, as now. In 1831 the illness of the steward resulted in Stockton's appointment temporarily, as steward of the institution,[8] an appointment which was permanently con-

[6] William S., 1830; Samuel, 1832; Francis Richard, 1834; John Drean, 1836; Marie Louise, 1838; William Snethen, 1841; Ann Virginia, 1846 (died early).

[7] *Truth versus "A Wesleyan Methodist," and Other Objectors; containing Remarks and Animadversions on a book entitled "Methodist Error," etc.* By a Lay-Member of the Methodist Episcopal Church. Phila., 1820.

[8] A record in the Minute Book of the Board of Directors of Blockley reads quaintly as follows: (Nov. 14, 1831) "Mr. Woolf presented the following minute

firmed at a meeting of the Board of Directors on December 26, 1831.

In 1834 Stockton supervised the transfer of the Philadelphia Almshouse to its new location in Blockley Township on the west bank of the Schuylkill River, the site now occupied by the Philadelphia General Hospital. From its location, then a considerable distance from the city proper, the designation "Blockley" became so common a reference to the Hospital that it has persisted to this day.

Throughout the years of his service at Blockley, until 1844, William Stockton continued his writing on matters of Methodist practice. He was a reformer of the sternest dye, and a man of inflexible convictions. Thus Thomas Hewlings Stockton, his son, tells of life in the Stockton household:

There was my humble home. The *Bible* was in it—the literary light of the world. My parents believed and studied it as the Book of God. They taught me to do the same. . . . The Sabbath, moreover, was hallowed there as I have seldom seen it elsewhere. Everything that could be done on Saturday, in preparation for it, was done. The house was full of stillness. Reading was more exclusively sacred. Conversation was more solemn. At church time, the door was locked, and parents, children, and the "hired girl," repaired to the place of public worship. All day cooking was avoided, as far as practicable. It was a day of bodily rest, of spiritual enjoyment and improvement.[9]

During the years that followed, Stockton became more deeply involved in church affairs, becoming in fact the leader in a schism within the Methodist Church, upon the matter of

of the Committee of the House in relation to the Steward, with the resolution which was adopted by the Board.

"Whereas the Steward of this house by reason of indisposition is unable at present to fulfill the duties of his station, and the situation of the house requiring a person to have the General Superintendence in all its various departments (except such as are especially entrusted to the matron) and the Committee having selected Wm. S. Stockton, the Agent, to act as Steward until otherwise ordered, therefore,

"*Resolved,* that this board concur in the selection and approve of the measure adopted by the Committee of the house in relation thereto."

[9] *Poems: with Autobiographic and other Notes,* Phila., 1862, pp. 292–293.

lay-representation in church government, which resulted in the formation of the Methodist Protestant Church.

In the early years of his administration of Blockley, William Stockton seems to have been efficient and conscientious. The records of the hospital are terse and businesslike, and only occasionally during the years of his service is any mention made of him, but routine reports to the Board of Directors, signed by Stockton, appear frequently. In 1844 he was dismissed as Superintendent of Blockley, after seventeen years of service to the institution. The circumstances surrounding this dismissal are curious, in the light of William Stockton's character. In 1839 an investigation into the accounts for the preceding year revealed that abnormal quantities of foodstuffs were purchased—far more than the patients could possibly have consumed. One item alone showed that over fifty-four thousand pounds of meat were not accounted for. It is quite clear that William Stockton did not profit by any of the dishonest trafficking in institutional supplies. Indeed, no charge other than lack of supervision was brought against him. The severest indictment of his stewardship says only that

The utter lack of discipline and the mis-management of the institution were very apparent during the time that Steward Stockton had charge. There was not a proper supervision of the internal affairs and the subordinate officials seemed to be allowed to do as they saw fit. If the steward possessed the authority he should have had, and it is to be presumed that he had, the abuses that existed could not have continued if proper vigilance had been organized. There appeared to be entirely too much dependence placed upon men who were unworthy of it.[10]

Shortly after this report was made the time to elect the steward and other officials arrived. Six members voted for the re-election of Mr. Stockton as Steward, and it seemed as if they were determined to sustain him whether he was right or wrong.

A number of ballots were taken, and, as no person received a majority of the votes, it was found to be impossible to elect a Steward at that meeting, and the old Steward was instructed by

[10] Charles Lawrence, *The History of Almshouses and Hospitals in Philadelphia*, Philadelphia, 1905, p. 154.

a resolution to continue to perform the duties of the office until a successor could be elected.

The gentlemen who voted for Mr. Stockton were John Price Wetherill, Peter-a-Keyser, William S. Hansell, John Keefe, Michael Andress, and John Hemphill, and as they were all citizens of standing in the community there must have been some reason for their action, although it was not explained in the minutes.[11]

William Stockton continued to serve from this time (1839) until June 24, 1844, when the Board of Directors accepted his resignation. Stockton's inefficiency as an administrator, which appeared only in the last few years of his stewardship at Blockley, may have been caused by his growing preoccupation with religion and the writing of religious polemics. Discounting the filial piety, and the florid style characteristic of such writing at the period, the statement of Stockton's eldest son, Thomas, is illuminating:

Notwithstanding many cares and anxieties, and the pressure of civil duties for the prolonged term of seventeen years, it may be said of him, with all propriety, that for about forty years, in whole, so far as laymen are concerned and the specialty of Church Government, he was *the* Methodist writer of America, if not of the world. I think it likely that during that time he wrote more largely on that subject than all the laymen of Methodism combined, and more wisely than the great majority of its ministers. This was his ruling passion; or rather, his providential mission.[12]

Certainly William Stockton's life gives full evidence of his preoccupation with unworldly things. His early days as grocery and as bookstore clerk, his mature years as Superintendent of Blockley—never at a large salary—and his early retirement from any further pursuit of this world's goods, to write voluminous tracts in the causes of Methodism and Temperance (i.e., total abstinence) indicate clearly his intense zeal for religion. His mother, fortunately, owned a large farm on North Broad Street[13] and was able to provide generously for her son and his large family.

11 *Ibid.*, p. 149.
12 Thomas Stockton, *op. cit.*, pp. 312–313.
13 The site now occupied by Temple University.

In his adult years Frank Stockton never entered a church, save as a courtesy on the occasion of a wedding or a funeral. Religion was a subject to which he seldom alluded, and the conclusion is inescapable that the zeal of his father had much to do with his quiet revolt against the stern rigors of conscientious Methodism.

Mrs. Stockton, Frank's mother, was of a different mold, and it is probably from her that much of his imaginative faculty came. A practical woman, devoted to her husband's interests, she had also gaiety and an unwearying interest in her children. She read them stories, she kept them quiet while their father wrote his never-ending tracts, she fed hearty appetites on a slim budget, and she encouraged the developing skills of Frank and John and Louise in writing. It was she who, reared in a gentler tradition than her husband, encouraged the children to draw and to write. It was she who first gave Frank his affection for the South, and taught him tolerance. From what we know of William Stockton, it seems that Frank Stockton's kindness and broad human sympathy must have come from her. That she could establish a school for young ladies, when she was past middle age, and manage it successfully, speaks for her courage, her determination, and her practicality. If heredity offers any clue to Frank Stockton's abilities, the genes of his imaginativeness, humor, and intelligent practicality came from his mother.

Chapter II

ON April 5, 1834, Francis Richard Stockton was born in the Superintendent's new quarters at Blockley. He was the third child of William Stockton's second marriage, the others—William S., and Samuel—having died in infancy. Through some unfortunate circumstance, Frank Stockton was born with one leg shorter than the other, an infirmity which materially affected his later life.[1]

A story, largely apocryphal, is told that his half-sister, Emily Louisa, a young woman with a deep interest in the more romantic aspects of history, suggested that the new baby be named Francis Richard, after Francis I of France, and Richard Cœur de Lion. The story seems unnecessarily romantic, since Richard was a traditional name in the Stockton family, and a half-brother, born in 1815, had been named Francis Asbury. However, since there is also a belief in the family that Frank's younger sister, Marie Louise (1838), was named after the second wife of Napoleon, the story may have some foundation in fact.

Through infancy and early childhood Stockton lived in the Steward's quarters at Blockley, with the family of half-brothers and sisters, and the increasing number of his own brothers and sisters. John Drean was born in 1836, Marie Louise in 1838, and William Snethen Stockton in 1841.

In 1840 Frank went to school. He attended the Zane Street School at 713 Filbert Street, since his family had moved to 509 Spruce Street. There are no records of his activities during his grammar-school days, and Stockton himself, in later years, volunteered no information. One fact only emerges, that

[1] Some accounts attribute his lameness to an injury sustained in childhood. Mrs. Wm. McAllister, source of the above statement, stated clearly that Stockton's lameness was congenital.

Stockton early revealed an impish pleasure in giving pets absurdly long names. The name of his dog, "Fax Mentis Incendium Gloria."—"Fax" for short—parallels closely his later naming of a favorite horse "David Douglas—15A Castle Street —Edinburgh—Scotland" [2]—"David" for short.

In February 1848 Stockton entered Central High School. Central High School, then located on the east side of Juniper below Market Street, opposite Centre Square,[3] had been founded in 1838. Already, however, it had established itself as an integral part of Philadelphia civic life, drawing to its classrooms the better students from all the city's grade schools.

In 1848 high-school training was about the equivalent of our present lower division college course. Indeed, the charter of Central High School carried with it the authority to grant academic degrees, and its curriculum closely approximated that of the average Junior college of today. Already, too, it had a fine faculty, many of whose members later became distinguished scholars and educators.

The record of Stockton's attendance at Central High School reads briefly: "Frank R. Stockton (#1574) admitted February, 1848 (aged 13 yrs., 10 mos.); left February, 1852, member 19th class." [4]

Some indication of the type of student at Central High School in 1848 may be gathered from the names of a few of Stockton's classmates and associates who became prominent in politics, letters, law, and medicine: as classmates, there were the Hon. James T. Mitchell, Chief Justice, Supreme Court of Pennsylvania; John Aylmer Dorgan, the poet; George Inman Riche, fourth President of Central High School; while during his four-year course he came into association with the Hon. William H. Ashman, Judge of the Orphan's Court of Philadelphia, and a life-long friend; James G. Barnwell, philanthropist; Samuel S. Fisher, U.S. Commissioner of Patents; P. A. B. Widener, financier; and Dr. W. W. Keen, surgeon.

2 This was the name of his English publisher, and the horse was purchased with the first check received from him for stories published abroad.

3 The present site of City Hall.

4 General Catalogue, Central High School, 1838–1890, Phila., 1890.

These men are representative of the type of student characteristic of Central High School at this period. The course of study was academic, embracing English, French, History, Chemistry, General Science, Classical Languages, together with special studies in Anglo-Saxon, Anatomy, Phonography, and Book-keeping.[5]

One of Stockton's early ambitions was to study medicine, and much of his class work was devoted to the sciences, physics and chemistry particularly. Although he abandoned his desire to be a physician, his interest in physical phenomena never left him, and revealed itself frequently in his writing in later years. He was a realist, preferring always the concrete fact to the romantic and remote ideal.

Clearly revealed during these high-school years are the qualities which shaped his career as a writer. Even in his adolescence, he was a logician; not, perhaps, in the sense of formal dialectics, but certainly in the sense of one who lucidly pursues logical sequences. His class exercises, several examples of which are still preserved by his niece, reveal these qualities, and reveal, too, a facility of expression unusual in a boy of sixteen. The exercises are written in a neat, immature hand, embellished with the chirographical flourishes so common to the time. The covers of his copy books are inscribed with artistically executed scrolls and conventionalized designs, within which the title of the exercise, the class for which it was prepared, and his name, *Frank R. Stockton*, were lettered. He possessed uncommon skill with the pen, and the craftsmanship he later exhibited as a wood engraver must have shown itself early. Its development was in great part due to his inability to participate in the more robust activities of boys of his age, and although Stockton was no adolescent recluse like Henry Blake Fuller, he must have spent many hours sitting at the dining-room table, quietly at work on his lessons, drawing, lettering, or writing down his early fancies.

Physical activity for Stockton was limited to the daily walks

[5] In 1848, "Education" as a science of pedagogy had not been developed, so that it was entirely possible to attend high school without interfering with one's education.

to and from school. It was his habit during these walks "to take up the thread of a plot and carry it on from day to day until the thing became a serial story." [6] Such a daily exercise, with its training of memory, developed materially that extraordinary ability he possessed which enabled him to think out fully an entire story, including dialogue, before he put a word on paper or dictated a sentence to his amanuensis. It must have been of this time, too, that he spoke in later life:

I was very young when I determined to write some fairy tales because my mind was full of them. I set to work, and in course of time, produced several which were printed. These were constructed according to my own ideas. I caused the fanciful creatures who inhabited the world of fairy-land to act, as far as possible for them to do so, as if they were inhabitants of the real world. I did not dispense with monsters and enchanters, or talking beasts and birds, but I obliged these creatures to infuse into their extraordinary actions a certain leaven of common sense.[7]

Stockton possessed the imaginative faculty so necessary to the accomplished story-teller, but it was an imagination checked by a logical perception of realities. It was, indeed, this linking of the world of fantasy with the real world which gave his writing its individuality. Like Chesterton of a later day, Stockton delighted in viewing the absurd and the incongruous and the impossible with a grave, if puckish, wonderment at the essential rightness of the topsy-turvy.

It is a common practice of biographers to dwell at length upon the youthful environment, the developing characteristics of their subjects; to see influences where they exist, if they exist at all, only potentially. It is not necessary with Stockton. By the time he was nineteen, his character was fully determined, and although the years brought maturity of judgment, mental development, and crystallization of his abilities, his character remained, in any essential, unchanged.

While still a student at Central High School, Stockton won

---

[6] *McClure's,* November, 1893, p. 467.

[7] "A Memorial Sketch of Mr. Stockton," by Mrs. F. R. Stockton, in *A Bicycle of Cathay; The Shenandoah Edition of the Novels and Stories of Frank R. Stockton,* Vol. XXIII, p. 192. Cf., also, *The Captain's Toll Gate,* Appleton, 1903.

a prize for a story submitted in a contest held by the *Boys' and Girls' Journal.*[8] This was his first appearance in print, according to legend.

His brother John, two years younger, and destined later to edit the Philadelphia *Post,* shared with him his interest in writing. Together they composed stories, and read them to their mother, and their wide-eyed sister, Louise. Once when some poetry they had written was rejected by the editor of a Baltimore religious paper, they gravely decided that editors could not recognize poetry when they saw it. To prove it, they copied a few lines from Milton's *Paradise Regained* and mailed it to the undiscriminating editor. He printed it, to their mild consternation, and proved that, if he did not know Milton, he did know poetry.

Toward the end of his high-school course, Stockton was regularly submitting stories to editors and, like most novices, was as regularly collecting rejection slips. In his later success, he was able to sell so many of his early stories, reworked, that not many unpublished manuscripts exist. One of these few unpublished stories was obviously written at this period. It is entitled "The First Beefsteak," and is written on a theme similar to Lamb's "Dissertation on Roast Pig." It describes how Adam and Eve accidentally discover that broiled cow is delicious. The transparent little tale, juvenile in conception, is full of immature and precious descriptions of Nature in her more benevolent moods. But Stockton worked diligently, and the improvement in matter and manner in the remaining manuscripts is evident.

He was graduated from Central High School in February 1852, with the degree of Bachelor of Arts. Immediately after his graduation, he began his apprenticeship as a wood engraver, while his brother John studied steel engraving. To young men of the Stocktons' manual skill, both these crafts offered lucrative futures, since editors were beginning to use illustrations to make the format of their papers more attractive

---

[8] This story, mentioned by several biographers of Stockton, has not been found. Stockton ignored it in his own reference to his first published story.

to the eye, and modern methods of halftone reproduction were yet to be invented.

While he was learning his craft, Stockton did not neglect his writing. An unpublished manuscript gives us a picture unconsciously autobiographical. It is entitled "What Can I Do for an Old Gentleman?" and it tells the story of a young man, Tom Eden, who has literary ambitions, and just enough money to keep him in New York for one year. After eight months of fruitless effort to achieve editorial recognition, he finds himself with four dollars and eighty-two cents, and the unpleasant prospect of returning home, acknowledging himself a failure to his practical-minded family, and accepting a stool as clerk in the family business.

In the manuscript of "What Can I Do for an Old Gentleman?" Stockton has pasted several printed rejection slips, only one of which—from *Appleton's Journal*—is recognizable, since the firm names have been neatly clipped out, and fictitious ones inserted.

Tom Eden's desperate search begins. He seeks an old gentleman who will give him a job in return for extraordinary services, but he wisely rules out the possibilities of drowning daughters and runaway horses as being improbable sources of the introduction he desires. Tom finds his old man, gets his job, through the medium of a planchette, which reunites a long-separated family.

"What Can I Do for an Old Gentleman?" is discursive, slow-moving, and it is written in that extended style characteristic of Stockton in most of his early stories. But it contains a significant passage which indicates that he understood very clearly what he wished to do:

It may be as well to state that the pursuit in life which Tom considered himself so well qualified to follow was Literature—his ideas, however, were somewhat peculiar,—and he thought philosophical. His wants being few and his tastes rural, he intended after he had made himself sufficiently known in the Literary world, to retire to some country place, (not his native village) and there enjoy life at such expense of money and labor as would be far below the average amount necessary to support his fellow men—as his reputation and remuneration increased, he would travel—what more need he? Give him pen and ink—some paper, and just enough fame to command attention to his articles, and he had in his hand the true purse of Fortunatus. Tom wished to enjoy life as he worked, not after his work was done, and he was by no means a fool—so he tried Literature. Everyone knows there are two ways by which a man can make money by the joint labor of his brain and pen. One, is to learn the business, as you would a trade, and become a journalist, employed by those who will harness your Pegasus, but will at the same time provide him with oats—the other is to write what one pleases, as one pleases, and endeavour to find someone who will also be pleased with it, and—pay for it.[9]

It is interesting to note how closely Stockton's later life approximated the ideal set forth here in a manuscript written before he was twenty.

Frank and John Stockton opened an engraver's shop together, when they had learned their trades. One of Frank's advertisements is reproduced on the opposite page.

Stockton supported himself, and probably contributed materially to the support of his family, by his wood engraving for many years, for it was not until after 1870 that his literary work brought in any appreciable amount of money. Among other work, he cut the seven illustrations for the volume of poetry published by his half-brother, the Rev. Thomas H. Stockton, in 1862.[10] Two of these were original concepts of his own, one of them, "The City Sunset," having something of the quality of brooding spaciousness of Doré, although the execution is less deft, the draughtsmanship lacking in assured finish.

During the years, then, between his graduation from Central High School in 1852 and the publication of his first mature story in 1855, Stockton was developing his trade as wood engraver, and writing to learn to write. His father had retired;

[9] Pp. 2–3, unpublished MS, in possession of Mrs. George E. Cantrell, Haddonfield, N.J.

[10] Poems, with Autobiographic and Other Notes, Phila., 1862.

Frank R. Stockton,

ENGRAVER

on

WOOD.

SOUTH-WEST CORNER OF SIXTH AND CHESTNUT STREETS,

PHILADELPHIA.

Every Variety of Illustration of Letter-press,

VIEWS OF BUILDINGS AND MACHINERY.

Engravings for Patentees, for Catalogues of Stock, &c. &c. &c.

Carefully Executed from PHOTOGRAPHS and DRAWINGS.

VIRGINIA WATER.

his brother John had begun his career of successful journalism, and his mother was establishing herself as the mistress of a select school for young ladies. The Stockton family fortunes were rising, and Frank Stockton himself was about to experience the thrill of seeing his first printed story published in the same year that he attained his legal majority.

Chapter III

ON Saturday, September 1, 1855, Frank Stockton's first published story appeared in the Philadelphia *American Courier*.[1] The *American Courier*, as its six-column streamer announced, was "devoted to Literature, News, Science, The Arts, Mechanics, Agriculture, The Markets, Education, Morals, Health, Amusement, etc." Stockton's story is entitled "The Slight Mistake; or How M. de la Renardelle happened to be in the 'Garde,'" and its authorship, cryptically, is credited to "The G.W.M."[2] It is a good story beginning:

In the year 16—, in the city of Paris, in the back parlor of the "Oiseau d'Or," around a table, were seated four gentlemen, who, by their brilliant uniforms and huge mustachios, might easily be recognized as soldiers of the 'Garde.'

This is quite in the tradition of the French romance, but the story has more to recommend it than that—it has pace, and vivacity. Stockton introduces "the four gentlemen" in this exuberant fashion:

First then, we will notice the tall, bony veteran, with his tremendous mustache twisted into the most recherché points, and his left cheek disfigured by a long scar. That is Captain Alexis de Verney, and he gained his scar at Rocroi a dozen years before. The fat gentleman on his right is Major Dusonbierres, who can tell of more feats of valor than Captain Alexis ever performed. The fine looking man at the head of the table, is Doctor Solotre, one of the beaux of the army, whose eyes and prescrip-

---

[1] *The American Courier; A Family Newspaper: Neutral in Politics and Religion*, ed. by Andrew McMakin, Vol. 25, No. 27.

[2] Stockton himself is the source of this information. A letter in the Pierpont Morgan Library, New York, addressed to Mr. Laurens Maynard, reads: "My first published writing was a story called 'A Slight Mistake' (an imitation of Dumas and other favorite French authors) and was printed in McMakin's 'American Courier,' Philadelphia, September 1, 1855."

tions do equal execution, and who prides himself on being able to drink two bottles of the landlord's 'oldest,' after the Captain and the Major are under the table. Finally, the tall, broad-shouldered youth, who tips back his chair, is Lieutenant Henri Armand de la Renardelle, de Carmantois, who can employ three bottles more than the Doctor, and then carry him home.

The other three gentlemen of the Garde serve as an audience for the story of M. de la Renardelle. Henri, son of a land-poor Breton nobleman, is sent by his father to Troiteur, the estate of his wealthy uncle. He takes down the family heirloom, the long sword of his great grandfather "Adolphus the Strong," and with Felix, a solemn family retainer, sets forth. But not until he has "embraced my father once, my mother twice, and the gardener's daughter three times."

At Troiteur he meets his rich, jolly uncle, and his uncle's ward, the beautiful Mademoiselle de la Leume. Henri falls in love immediately, and from this point forward is pictured as one of those mildly simple lovers whom Stockton delighted in drawing. Asked by the lovely Marie to guard an arbor in which she was preparing a secret, Henri bares the gleaming sword of Adolphus, and takes up a position nearby. But curiosity over-whelms him, and, stealthily approaching the hidden bower, he discovers his loved one in deep conversation with his ap-parent rival, M. de Gregoire. Angered by Mademoiselle Marie's seeming duplicity, Henri precipitates a duel with M. de Gregoire early the next morning, and wounds him in the shoulder. Marie, learning of this attack, sends for Henri, and tells him that M. de Gregoire, as an old family friend, had been deputized by her guardian to obtain her consent to marriage with Henri, an alliance desired by both his uncle and his father. Henri at last realizes that he had been sent to Troiteur to fall in love with Marie. The "slight mistake" explains Henri's presence in the *Garde* and is an explanatory prelude to his announcement that Mademoiselle is going to be married "to one who is a little more sensible than he used to be." It explains, also, his application for leave of absence for the next week.

"The Slight Mistake" is a gay story, and if its plot is slight, it has a real person in the character of Henri, and a flesh-and blood heroine in the Mademoiselle de la Leume. There is a quixotic humor in Henri's courageous defense of the frightened Marie when she is attacked by a bull:

When the bull ran *from* her towards the other ladies, I had not stirred; when he turned towards her, I leaped from the fence, and drawing my sword and dropping the hoptoad, I shouted "À Carmantois! À Carmantois!" at the same time rushing upon the enemy. It did not take long for my vigorous legs to bring me to the place of action. Just as the bull's horns were within a yard of his intended victim, I reached him, and with a tremendous sweep of my sword, at one blow I cut off his—tail!

The calm, realistic recital of absurdity which first appears in "The Slight Mistake" was a method which Stockton was to develop into the distinguished artistry of *Rudder Grange* and *The Casting Away of Mrs. Lecks and Mrs. Aleshine.*

His determination to become a successful author having been strengthened by this appearance in print, Stockton continued to labor with wood block and burin—and the pen. No record of any story in print has been discovered, however, until "Kate" was published in *The Southern Literary Messenger* in December 1859. "Kate" is the recital of an idyllic summer love affair, in which the hero, an ineffectual, well-meaning soul, triumphs over the inevitable summer-colony strong man and wins his bride in spite of himself. It is written in a slow-moving, seemingly aimless style, and there is a strong accent on descriptions of woods and country landscapes, the setting in which Stockton himself was happiest. Kate is a charming girl, exasperatingly careful to keep her lover dangling miserably (and happily) until vacation is over.

That Stockton had his second story published in *The Southern Literary Messenger,* once edited by Edgar Allan Poe, and still one of America's leading literary periodicals, was a distinct achievement. As late as 1860, free-lance writing in America was financially hazardous. There were few bold enough to attempt to support themselves wholly by writing. Hawthorne had been successively a customs inspector and American consul at Liverpool; Longfellow was forty-seven, and a well-established writer, before he dared retire from teaching at Harvard to devote himself exclusively to his poetry. Yet independent writing—"to write what one pleases, as one pleases, and endeavor to find someone who will also be pleased with it, and—pay for it" [3]—seems to have been one of Stockton's earliest ambitions—an ambition he realized fully in later life.

In 1860, Stockton was twenty-six years old, and at the threshold of his successful career as a writer. He was a man of slight, almost frail, appearance, a slightness belied by broad shoulders and the powerful arms he had developed as a compensation for his malformed leg. He dressed somberly and, after the fashion of his time, wore a mustache which stood out rigidly some inches from the oval of his small, delicately-formed face. His complexion was dark,[4] his eyes clear, but already with those wrinkles at the corners which gave him a genial, warming expression. He smiled often, but when he laughed, although his shoulders shook, and his eyes almost closed, he laughed soundlessly, merely contorting his lips. The merriment was genuine, but this soundless laughter was a peculiarity which amazed those who met him for the first time. In his person, he was meticulously neat—a habit learned easily in a house full of brothers and sisters. But in 1860, there was for Stockton a special reason for scrupulous attention to externals.

Mrs. William Stockton, his mother, had established a school—the West Philadelphia School for Young Ladies—at 39th Street and Powelton Avenue, sometime after William Stockton's retirement from the world of debits and credits. To this school, as a teacher of literature, came Mary Ann Edwards Tuttle, of Georgetown, South Carolina. Miss Tuttle

---

[3] Stockton MS, "What Can I Do for an Old Gentleman?"

[4] According to Robert Underwood Johnson, Stockton "was the darkest man of the Caucasian race I have ever seen." *Remembered Yesterdays*, Boston, 1923, p. 104.

was a gracious woman, interested in literature, interested in travel, and possessed, in addition to physical comeliness, an alertness of mind which appealed to Stockton. Her teaching career at the West Philadelphia School for Young Ladies was short. They were married on April 30, 1860, in Burlington, New Jersey.

The Stockton marriage, although it was childless, seems to have been ideal. Throughout their long years together, Mrs. Stockton aided him in every way possible—acting as his amanuensis, reading to him when his eyes failed, collaborating with him, and, as a matter of daily course, smoothing the essential domestic details into an orderly and comfortable routine. In order to avoid confusion in the family, Mary Ann Stockton telescoped her name into "Marian," the name by which she was known to her intimates.

After their marriage, the Stocktons set out to find a country home which should be within their means, and within commuting distance of New York, where Frank had opened an engraving office at 160 Fulton Street.[5] It was while looking for a home in northern New Jersey that Stockton found the unique family, living on a canal boat on the Harlem River, which later gave him the inspiration for *Rudder Grange*.

A suitable location, in Nutley, New Jersey, was found, and the Stocktons, with an enthusiasm reflected later in their joint effort, *The Home*,[6] and in Stockton's story, "Our Fire Screen,"[7] set about the pleasant task of home making.

They had been married only a few months when Stockton's father suffered a fracture of the hip. He was seventy-five years old, and the broken bone would not mend; after lingering for three months in severe pain, he died on November 20, 1860.

Although it is evident that Stockton was making money as

[5] This New York venture was probably the result of Stockton's unsuccessful attempt to sell Jay Cooke's 7–30 bonds during the Civil War. For this interesting story of American finance, see Ellis Paxon Oberholtzer, *Jay Cooke, Financier of the Civil War*, 2 Vols., Philadelphia, 1907.

[6] *The Home—Where It Should Be and What to Put in It* (in Putnam's Handy-Book Series). G. P. Putnam & Sons, New York, 1873.

[7] *Novels and Stories*, Vol. XVI, p. 259.

a wood engraver—enough at least to make marriage possible—
he continued his writing. His story "Kate" had so impressed
the editor of *The Southern Literary Messenger* with his
ability that he offered Stockton thirty dollars for his next, more
ambitious tale, "A Story of Champaigne," which was announced in the "Editor's Table" of the magazine in November 1860:

In our next number, we shall give the first installment of an
interesting novelet, entitled "A Story of Champaigne." It is from
the pen of a new and successful aspirant for literary honors.

Stockton's "Story of Champaigne" did not appear in the
Messenger until January 1861, when the first installment was
printed. Subsequent installments appeared in the issues of
February, April, and May. The March issue for some reason
omitted the story.

When "A Story of Champaigne" appeared, Frank R. Stockton was twenty-seven. Like its predecessor in *The Southern
Literary Messenger,* it is a good story. The more deeply one
reads in Stockton's work, the more clearly is it realized that
he was an extraordinarily even writer. Like all authors, particularly those whose published work is as voluminous as
Stockton's, his stories are not of unvarying excellence. Some
few are works of pure "inspiration"—an indefinable word
which critics use when they mean that a great idea and a
writer's technical ability to express it are happily fused. Many
of Stockton's stories are obviously works of editorial inspiration, stories written at the request, and by the specifications, of
magazine editors. But unlike many authors whose work bulks
large on library shelves, Stockton has little apprentice work
which must be hastily dismissed by the sympathetic critic.

To those familiar with "A Story of Champaigne" it is unnecessary to point out its obvious resemblances to Dumas' *The
Three Musketeers.* The character of its hero, Rupert, son of
the impoverished Sieur de Lachandais, who sets out for Paris
to make a name for himself in the military service of Louis
XIV, parallels that of the youthful d'Artagnan setting out on

his white horse to make his name and fortune. Other similarities are readily apparent, but for all its superficial similarities,
Stockton wrote no slavish reproduction of *The Three Musketeers*. The author who could write "Ting-a-ling" takes a hand
in working out the destinies of his characters.

Rupert de Lachandais, setting out from his obscure provincial home for Paris, is jogging along the road when his passage
is barred by a truculent stranger who makes the preposterous
request that Rupert surrender his horse. Rupert, eager to try
his new sword, resists, and spurring his horse, runs down the
highwayman, injuring him severely. Compassionate, he dis-
mounts, and solicitously cares for his attacker. The stranger
reveals himself as a courier, bearing an important packet of
documents to Mademoiselle Celeste d'Estandeaux, whose estate is still some twelve miles distant. He begs Rupert to carry
the messages, so that she will receive them before nightfall.
Rupert obliges, but at the castle he receives a cold welcome,
until he meets Tiberius Caesar, a dwarf.

Tiberius is one of Stockton's happier creations, directly
transported from the land of Ting-a-ling to act as *deux ex
machina* in Champaigne. Tiberius leads Rupert to the cottage
where Celeste has imprisoned herself to escape the drunken
supervision of her guardian, Count Maurice. Rupert is treated
most churlishly when he presents the important papers, but
philosophically admires the moon-drenched landscape, and
goes to sleep on a bench in the corridor.

In the morning Tiberius reappears. Rupert is received by
Mademoiselle Celeste, who proves to be young and beautiful,
and profuse apologies are given him. After a long delayed
meal, he resumes his journey to Paris. He is overtaken by
Tiberius, who has decided to become Rupert's servant.

From this point forward, the story follows a conventional
enough pattern. In Paris, Rupert takes up the cause of Mademoiselle Celeste, discovers that she is being cheated out of her
estate by the cruel and rapacious Count Maurice, and, after
many adventures of a swashbuckling and decidedly hilarious
nature (for Rupert is a typical Stocktonian hero who is never

permitted to be completely heroic) restores to her her rightful heritage, and, we presume, assumes its management himself.

Many scenes in "A Story of Champaigne" are memorable, but none makes so happy a picture as the scene in which Tiberius Caesar, realizing that the Parisian lawyer has the will of Celeste's father, which makes Count Maurice heir to the estate, steathily enters the eminent jurist's library while he is at dinner and, in order to make sure that he has secured the right document, burns *all* the lawyer's papers in his own fireplace! Since the lawyer's cabinets include wills, mortgages, birth certificates, notes and legal titles to the estates of many of his clients, the pathetic spectacle of his discovery of their incineration is one of Stockton's rarer and finer pictures.

Another scene of interest, but for a different reason, is Stockton's description of Rupert's reaction to the news of the death of his father, the Sieur de Lachandais. Restraint, sure emotional effectiveness, and sincerity give the passage poignant vividness when one remembers that Stockton's own father died but a short time before the story was published.

"A Story of Champaigne" sets the tempo of many of Stockton's later stories. It is an "early" story, and, as we shall see, he had not yet found the finished medium for the expression of his highly individual material, but his narrative manner remains essentially unchanged. Now he speeds it up to tell the story of "The Lady, or the Tiger?"; now he slows it down to depict the leisurely ways of *The House of Martha;* again, it becomes deceptively droll to recount the adventures at *The Squirrel Inn;* still again, it painfully and tediously pursues *The Hundredth Man.* But nearly always Stockton writes with that placid objectivity and matter-of-factness which describes the most hair-raising adventure, the most ludicrous situation, the most amazing circumstance, and the simplest culinary detail with equal detachment. He is the conscious artist, creating his effects by skill and craftsmanship. He writes with what is apparently a scrupulous regard for detailed truth, and deftly conveys the impression that he lacks the ability to disassociate the important from the trivial, the astounding from the commonplace, the irregular from the rule. The result is a body of memorable stories.

About 1860, the impetus of the Abolition Movement in the North, and the growing bitterness in the South over the question of States' Rights, led to repeated demands for disruption of the Union. The issues of *The Southern Literary Messenger* which carried "The Story of Champaigne" carried also columns of vehement protest against the demands of the North, and repeated defenses of the institution of slavery. Humanitarian Abolitionist tracts stirred Southern apologists to write treatises on the moral justification and the economic necessity for slavery in the cotton-growing South. The plea for secession was heard more and more frequently.

During this time—and throughout the entire Civil War—Stockton's sympathies were divided. Mrs. Stockton was a South Carolinian, and through visits to her home before and after his marriage Stockton knew more of the South, and the actual conditions there, than most Northerners. His sympathies were with the South, too, on the issue of States' Rights. He did not favor slavery, but he knew that its evils were not what earnest Abolitionists or sentimentalists like Harriet Beecher Stowe painted them. When the war came, some idea of his torn allegiances may be gained from the incident in which his brother John, with a Northern regiment, met his wife's brother, fighting for the South, during Pickett's charge at Gettysburg.

The angry times of 1860 caused Stockton to write one of his few essays on controversial matters, "A Northern Voice for the Dissolution of the Union." [8] It was a pamphlet printed at his own expense, and was, in his own words, "an attempt to avert the impending conflict between the states by suggesting a form of compromise." Stockton's idea was simple. He suggested that those states which wished to secede be permitted to do so, and that the Union be formed only from those States which gave consent to union, on the

[8] "A Northern Voice for the Dissolution of the Union," printed for the author, Philadelphia, 1861.

principle that government gains its authority from the consent of the governed. When Fort Sumter fell on April 12,
1861, Stockton withdrew "A Northern Voice" from circula-
tion.

Three years later, in 1864, Stockton again essayed public
approval of his plan for secession for those states which
wished to secede, in an unpublished MS, "A Real Union,"
in which he argues that a real union cannot be gained "by
means of war—by putting down slavery in those states in
which it exists, and then compelling those states to re-enter
the Union under such terms as we may prescribe. This plan
has been tried. We need not dwell upon its failure— Let all
the states that are now free, or that wish to be so, stand together as the United States of America, excluding all others."

Throughout the war years 1861–65 Stockton remained
otherwise silent.[9] Unable to volunteer for active service himself, even if his naturally pacific temperament had permitted
such a course, he continued at his trade as wood engraver.
His intelligence and ingenuity were demonstrated by his invention of a wood engraver's tool which would cut parallel
lines in one operation, thus making for greater accuracy and
professional finish in the engraving. This tool was an adapta-
tion of the single cutter, having a fixed blade and a movable
blade which could be adjusted through a considerable range
to any desired spacing by means of a screw device. Letters
Patent for this graver were issued to him February 20, 1866.

The Stockton family in Philadelphia was not prospering,
and probably because his aid was needed, Frank Stockton
and his wife removed to Philadelphia for a time. In 1867
John Russell Young, John M. Carson, and John Drean Stockton, Frank's brother, founded a newspaper, *The Philadelphia
Post,* the first issue of which appeared October 17th as *The
Philadelphia Morning Post.* It is mentioned by several
chroniclers of Stockton's life that he wrote articles for his

[9] During the years from December 1, 1859, to July 4, 1863, a humorous
magazine, *Vanity Fair,* had a short existence. That Stockton contributed a
number of short sketches to this allegedly humorous periodical is most probable, although nothing of his can be identified with certainty.

brother's paper, but nothing in the files of the *Post* can be identified as his. It was, however, his first definite literary association, and from this time forward wood engraving became progressively less important. By 1870, Stockton had given up the burin and block altogether, and was occupied exclusively in writing and editorial work.

However vital the atmosphere of journalism may have been, it could hardly have assumed much of Stockton's interest, because he had already retired into that land of faëry whence he drew the inspiration for so much of his later work. When "Ting-a-ling" appeared in *The Riverside Magazine* in November and December, 1867, Stockton had found a happy outlet for the particular kind of fairy tales he had, as a youth, determined to write. Ting-a-ling, only an inch tall, but nevertheless the intimate of the local giant, is a charitable, persevering young elf. With the assistance of the giant in the more robust situations, Ting-a-ling exercises a benevolent supervision over the destinies of mere humans (with especial care for hapless princesses) who get themselves imprisoned in donjon-keeps, and who in other irrational fashions make themselves unhappy. An enterprising elf, Ting-a-ling has many adventures which he meets with resourcefulness and a stout heart. There was, for instance, the time he met the five magicians and, with their amiable assistance, utterly ruined the bad dwarf's party.[10] And there was that trip to Turilira,[11] which so taxed his endurance. Ting-a-ling's charm, and the expression of an altogether new note in children's stories,[12] persuaded a publisher to print a collection of his adventures in time for the Christmas trade of 1870.[13] It was Stockton's first appearance in book form. Many years later he wrote of this first appearance between covers: [14]

10 "Ting-a-ling and the Five Magicians," *Riverside Magazine,* Vol. III (February 1869), p. 57.

11 "Ting-a-ling's Visit to Turilira," *Riverside Magazine,* Vol. III (July 1869) p. 317.

12 Cf. Stockton's later expression of his serious purpose in creating these fanciful tales chiefly for adults who might be able to appreciate his delicate satire.

13 *Ting-a-ling* (Hurd and Houghton), Boston, 1870.

14 MS in possession of Mr. William A. McAllister, Westfield, New Jersey.

My first book was a long time in growing. It came up like a plant by the wayside of ordinary avocation, putting forth a few leaves at a time; and when at last it budded, there was good reason to doubt whether or not it really would blossom. At length, though, it did blossom, in red, brown, green and blue.

It was a book for young people, and was called *Ting-a-ling*. It was made up of fairy stories, and when these first went out, each by itself, to seek a place in the field of current literature, it was not at all certain that they would ever find such a place. The fairies who figured in these tales were not like ordinary fairies. They went, as it were, like strangers or foreigners, seeking admission in a realm where they were unknown and where their rights as residents were some time in being recognized.

I was far away in the backwoods of Virginia when I received the first copy of my first book, and what author has forgotten the first copy of his first book? Mine was of handsome proportions, bound in crimson cloth, and embellished with glittering plumes. It was delicately illustrated, beautifully printed, and I could imagine no home which would not be made brighter by the possession of the book, even if it were never read.

The unanimity of feeling in this respect between myself and the English speaking public was not immediately manifested, but I have always believed in the adage that, if you really want a thing done, you must do it yourself, and so, without reference to the duties of my fellow creatures, I performed my duty toward this book as far as I was able. Whenever my funds permitted it I bought a copy—at a discount—and presented it to a friend. It was gratifying to reflect that in this way a good many persons were made acquainted with these stories.

It is long since I have endeavored to infuse realism into fairyland, and if in a later work I have touched the real world with something of the fanciful and fantastic, it has received more favor than was given to my first transmutations of the imaginary and the real.

Side by side, Stockton was writing for his new-found audience in *Riverside,* and for the adult audience whose attention he wished to capture. For *Riverside,* to which he was now a steady contributor, he produced a series of juvenile tales and informative articles. A story for adults, "Mahala's

Drive," appeared in *Lippincott's Magazine* for November 1868. "Mahala's Drive" is a sentimental little episode, laid in the South, describing the part a loyal Negro servant plays in restoring a son to his family. It is interesting as Stockton's earliest treatment of the Negro character, and as a revelation of his understanding of the psychology of the Southern Negro.

In December 1868 a new magazine, *Hearth and Home,* made its appearance. It was edited by Mary Mapes Dodge, who had an established reputation as a writer of juvenile literature, and whose *Hans Brinker and the Silver Skates* is still a children's classic. Stockton was Mrs. Dodge's assistant and, together with George Cary Eggleston, also an assistant, he did much of the writing for each issue. Stockton's editorial position on *Hearth and Home* was a happy one in many ways. He gained valuable editorial experience, he was provided with a ready outlet for his writing, and the knowledge and reputation so gained ultimately resulted in his selection as assistant editor of *St. Nicholas Magazine* when that amazing periodical was founded.

Hearth and Home was not essentially a children's magazine. As its title indicates, it was intended to be a helpful, entertaining weekly magazine which would appeal to every member of the family. Stockton wrote, consequently, not only stories, but also short paragraphs on home decoration, dressmaking, topics of the day, preventive medicine, handicraft, and vermin control. He became so versatile in matters domestic that, noting that he had contributed to every department of the paper but the one devoted to the pet recipes of the contributors, he invented a dish, "Cold Pink":

Take up all the white meat left over from the Thanksgiving Turkey, and chop it up very fine. Pour a thin cranberry sauce over the cold meat. Mix well, put in a china form and set it away to get cold. When cold, serve.[15]

Mrs. Dodge accepted this culinary gem, and paid him for it at current rates, two dollars.

15 Quoted in *Author,* Vol. III (June 15, 1891), p. 89.

Of the many short tales of Stockton's which appeared in *Hearth and Home* during 1869–70, the story of "The Naiad and the Dryad, or The Whole Story of Little Bo-Peep's Sheep" [16] is particularly memorable. Quaintly, it presents some excellent and rational reasons why Miss Bo-Peep's sheep came home without their caudal appendages, a lamentable occurrence which is not fully particularized in the original. While writing such articles as "After Turtle's Eggs," [17] "Up a Tree," [18] and "The Deadly Sumach," [19] Stockton was gathering the kind of informative material he used in his next book, *Roundabout Rambles,* which he published in 1872.

Throughout his work on *Hearth and Home,* Stockton kept clearly before him his desire for a wide, and a mature, audience. He was gradually becoming known to editors, and that he was not tagged simply as a writer of juvenile fiction is attested by an announcement which appeared in the short-lived humorous magazine *Punchinello,* for November 1870, in which a story "by Frank R. Stockton" is promised for the next issue. But alas for *Punchinello* and Frank Stockton, the magazine died before the December issue. The promised story was "Stephen Skarridge's Christmas," which was afterward published in *Scribner's Magazine.*[20]

For his birthday in 1871, Mrs. Stockton gave her husband a copy of the *Dictionary of English Synonyms and Synonymous Expressions,*[21] a book to which he had frequent reference for the rest of his life. On the flyleaf is written, "Frank R. Stockton from Marian E. Stockton, April 5, 1871. Rebound, August, 1887. Rebound, October, 1903."

The friendly relationship between *Scribners*—at that time *Scribner, Armstrong and Co.*—and Stockton, a relationship which was shortly to affect his fortunes considerably, was productive of Stockton's second book, *Roundabout Rambles*

[16] *Hearth and Home,* Vol. II (August 6, 1870), p. 525.
[17] *Ibid.,* October 30, 1869.
[18] *Ibid.,* February 12, 1870.
[19] *Ibid.,* September 24, 1870.
[20] *Scribner's Magazine,* o.s. Vol. III (January 1872), p. 279.
[21] B. R. Soule, Boston, 1871.

in Lands of Fact and Fancy.[22] The volume was given hand-some format, and was profusely illustrated. A Prussian blue cloth cover, decorated in black and gold after the rococo fashion of the day, gave it a handsome appearance. Working in collaboration with his illustrators,[23] Stockton wrote sixty-nine short articles of varying lengths, dealing with natural phenomena, freaks of geography and geology, curious animals, insect life, magical illusions, and entertaining examples of the physical properties of matter. *Roundabout Rambles,* in much of its scientific material—and Stockton was a precisionist in such details—is definitely dated today. But the book is interesting for another reason. If, as occurred at times, his stories contained a moral, the moral is always the outcome of some absurd and humane observation of life; he never felt called upon to lead his readers to righteousness. The only morals pointed out in *Roundabout Rambles* consist of mild Stocktonian admonitions to keep off railroad trestles, not to swing on church bells, and to observe a decent respect for the privacy of bees and the business ends of donkeys. Usually, too, some practical philosophy is reduced to homely terms, as in "Tickled by a Straw" [24] which is worth quoting here for another reason—it is one of the rare occasions in which Stockton wrote in verse.

TICKLED BY A STRAW

From his dreams of tops and marbles,
    Where the soaring kites he saw,
Is that little urchin wakened,
    Tickled by a wheaten straw.

[22] *Roundabout Rambles in Lands of Fact and Fancy,* Scribner, Armstrong & Co., New York, 1872.

[23] It is a curious circumstance that Stockton, with his very genuine skill, and his experience in wood engraving, then in general use for illustrations, never illustrated any of his own books. Who better than he could have visualized Pomona, or Mrs. Aleshine?

[24] *Op. cit.,* p. 305.

How do you suppose he likes it,
    Young one with annoying paw?
If I only were your mother,
    I'd tickle you with birchen straw.

Soon enough, from pleasant dreaming,
    You'll be wakened by the law,
Which provides for every vision
    Some sort of provoking straw.

In dreams of play, or hope, or loving,
    When plans of happiness you draw,
Underneath *your* nose may wiggle
    Life's most aggravating straw.

Later in the same year, in collaboration with Mrs. Stockton, he wrote a slim volume for *Putnam's Handy Book Series*. It was called *The Home—Where It Should Be and What to Put in It*.[25]

It was intended as a handbook, and covers such subjects as "The Location of the Home," "Furnishing the House," "Heating the House," and "Keeping the House." Although *The Home* was intended as a serious treatise, and no thought of humor entered Stockton's mind, the book is written in so stilted and pedantic a manner that its outmoded instructions make genuinely humorous reading today. What, for instance, might soap manufacturers think of this description of washday when their advertisements claim to make soiled clothes clean by a process combining the principles of imitative magic and osmosis, so that the laundress may use the day—or the major portion of it—for bridge or the movies?

Tuesday: As soon as the breakfast is served, the boiler must be removed to the front of the stove. When the water boils, put into it half a teacup of washing fluid, and a piece of hard soap, about two inches square, cut into shavings. Put in the fine clothes, and boil them twenty minutes. Take them out with as little water

[25] *The Home—Where It Should Be and What to Put in It*, G. P. Putnam & Sons, New York, 1873.

as possible, and without wringing, put into clear, cold water. If there are any soiled spots remaining on the clothes, they should be rubbed out before wringing from this water into the bluing water. The tub of bluing water is set near the other, so that the articles shall fall into it from the wringer.

Put your second division of clothes into the boiler, in the same water from which the fine things were taken and repeat the same process; but, if you have a third boiler full, it will be better to prepare fresh water.

Take the clothes out of the blue water, and rinse in cold, soft water, wring out, and hang out to dry.

With this plan of washing, and fair weather, the clothes will all be hung out by noon, unless the wash is very large, and the servant will have the afternoon for cleaning up the kitchen and washroom, putting away the tubs, boiler, etc., and making herself tidy. In the evening, the fine clothes and most of the starched things are to be sprinkled and folded, ready for ironing, and the bread is to be "set" for the next day's baking.

If *The Home* has no importance today, it still has interest because of the references to it in the early pages of *Rudder Grange*. In an appendix is supplied a list of the household items necessary to furnish a home completely which could be purchased for a thousand dollars. It is of this list that Euphemia's Husband remarked that he thought Euphemia had listed the *best* things at the *lowest* prices, a concept which went far to explain Euphemia's mentality and their difficulty in furnishing Rudder Grange according to their own book. It is but another evidence of Stockton's habit of writing out of his own immediate experience—a method of working from the particular to the general which is, incidentally, shared by every writer whose work has any claim to permanence.

The chronicle of Frank R. Stockton's life is sometimes an exasperating story because, like all good men, he led a placid and industrious life. For the annotating observer, therefore, there are few moments from which he can make spectacular chapter headings. But there are compensations. One of them is Stockton's association with *St. Nicholas Magazine*.

So remarkable had been the success of *Hearth and Home*

and the many similar publications, that Scribners determined
to launch a periodical which would make a specific appeal to
young people. The concept was magnificent. Periodicals had
been written exclusively for children before, but none had
ever conceived the simple plan of treating the young as intelligent beings. Magicians, practising legerdemain, had long
considered children their greatest hazard, since children in-
variably attended to the *substance* of their illusions, disre-
garding the patter upon which the magicians depended to
distract the more mature mind from their manipulations.
They made, therefore, a distinct appeal to children, and if
their motive was pragmatic, it was, by the same token, com-
mendable. Magazine editors, however, harboring adult ideas
of instructing the young, set about moral edification with
such fervor that parents approved heartily of their publications, and children sedulously avoided them. *St. Nicholas
Magazine* made an immediate and direct appeal. Children
waited eagerly for the next issue, it was so chock-full of interesting things. It is no exaggeration to say that it marked
another milestone in the cultural progress of American youth.
The list of contributors to its many volumes reads today like
a roll-call of all the better known and best loved authors of
the period in England and America. When Scribners
launched the magazine in 1873 they selected Mary Mapes
Dodge as its first editor. A woman of many interests, she
made an arrangement whereby she need appear in the office
of *St. Nicholas* only once a week, and someone was needed,
therefore, with authority to direct the destinies of the new
magazine. Stockton had already established himself securely
in *Hearth and Home,* and had given evidence of his editorial and executive ability. The post of assistant editor of
St. Nicholas was offered to him. He accepted. His associate
on *Hearth and Home,* George Cary Eggleston, was selected
as editor of that publication upon the retirement of Mrs.
Dodge and Stockton.

This arrangement by which Mrs. Dodge devoted only one
day a week to *St. Nicholas* threw a great burden on Frank

Stockton. He virtually edited the magazine. So great did the necessity for turning out copy become that he was forced to write, in some months, several articles himself. In order to avoid giving the impression that *St. Nicholas* was a one-man magazine, Stockton adopted two pseudonyms. He wrote as "Paul Fort" and "John Lewees," in the former *nom-de-plume* using the name of his younger brother, Paul, and in the latter the given name of his brother John, with a variant spelling of the name of his sister Louise.

His first story under the name of "Paul Fort" has an amusing resemblance to Benjamin Franklin's conclusion in "The Whistle." "Tommy Hopper's Choice" presents Tommy in the harassing position of having twenty-five cents all at once. He prices various desirable articles, but discovers that for some things even a whole quarter-dollar is not enough. Finally he buys twenty-five cents worth of peanuts, and receives an embarrassment of riches. He philosophically comes to the conclusion that "twenty-five cents in some places is too little, and, in some places, it's too much," a principle of economics the knowledge of which is sometimes valuable.

In the first issue of *St. Nicholas* Stockton began the publication of a long story which later had considerable popularity when it appeared in book form. "What Might Have Been Expected" [26] is significant chiefly as another of Stockton's earlier treatments of the southern darky. The characters of "Aunt Matilda" and "Uncle Braddock" are genuine. They reflect Stockton's acute observation of the southern Negro, glimpsed only in his infrequent trips to the home of Mrs. Stockton in the South. His sharply etched portraits of the pickaninnies, too, provoke a smile, so clearly and sympathetically has he pictured them.

The methods by which Tom Lauden and his sister Kate [27] achieve the economic security of the aged and infirm Aunt Matilda exhibit Stockton's ingenuity in episode-structure. And his methods of changing names—again evidenced many

[26] *What Might Have Been Expected*, Dodd & Mead, New York, 1874.

[27] Note Stockton's fondness for "Kate," a name he has given a number of his young, attractive feminine characters.

times in later work—is demonstrated by his laying the scene of the story in *Akeville*, a town which appears on the map of Virginia as Paineville.[28]

During 1874, Stockton continued his work as assistant editor of *St. Nicholas*, contributing articles and stories, supervising its editorial department, and generally seeing to it that the magazine went to press fully up to the high standard which had been set. That he did not reserve his sense of humor wholly for his literate public is evidenced by a story still fresh in the minds of those who remember him.[29] One rainy day Mrs. Dodge came to the editorial offices wearing rubbers, but upon her departure forgot them. Stockton, seeing them beside the desk, wrapped them carefully, called a messenger, and had them delivered immediately, together with a printed rejection slip of *St. Nicholas*. Underlined in ink were the words: "Many articles must be returned for reasons which have no connection with their literary merit."

[28] See also, *The Casting Away of Mrs. Lecks and Mrs. Aleshine*, Note, p. 93.
[29] Notably the late W. F. Clarke of Scarsdale, associated with Stockton, and later editor of *St. Nicholas*, who recounted the story.

Chapter IV

STOCKTON'S work on *St. Nicholas* contributed in great measure to the success of that magazine. The movies and regulated athletics fill, to a great extent, the leisure of the modern child; but these things did not exist in the seventies and eighties, and *St. Nicholas* exerted a powerful influence on the children of the last decades of the nineteenth century. At each year's end, the issues were sent away to be bound, and the beautiful red volumes were stored with other treasured volumes—the Bible, Shakespeare's plays, and Charles Dickens' novels. And no wonder! Its writers were such men as William Cullen Bryant, John Hay, Bret Harte, Joaquin Miller, Thomas Bailey Aldrich, H. C. Bunner, Mark Twain, Rudyard Kipling, William Dean Howells, Brander Matthews, Lewis Carroll, G. A. Henty, Louisa Alcott, Dan Beard, and Horatio Alger. Of them all, none was more happily placed than Frank Stockton himself, so voluminous was the material he contributed under his own and his two pen names. Writing under these three names—Stockton, Fort, Lewees—he produced a stream of stories and articles for *St. Nicholas,* and while they vary in quality from "What Might Have Been Expected," [1] a story of juvenile adventure with some excellent characterizations, to the slight moral tales like "Tommy Hopper's Choice," [2] the level of production and interest was uniformly high. Many of his articles were purely informative, like "Some Balloon Experiences" [3] and "Our Largest Friends," [4] and Stockton seems to have established distinct literary personalities for "Paul Fort" and "John Lewees," by

[1] *St. Nicholas,* Vol. I (November 1873–October 1874).
[2] *Ibid.,* Vol. I (November 1873), pp. 4–6. (Paul Fort)
[3] *Ibid.,* Vol. IX (November 1881), p. 30. (John Lewees)
[4] *Ibid.,* Vol. IX (September 1882), p. 838. (John Lewees)

publishing under the former name only slight, often unmotivated episodes, and under the latter chiefly informative articles. His better work he published under his own name. Anyone who has attempted to write stories for children will recognize in all Stockton's *St. Nicholas* stories that peculiar quality of directness and simplicity which only great writers can attain, and will recognize, too, his intuitive avoidance of the patronizing or moralistic tone which is not only inartistic, but dull. Perhaps much of the really phenomenal popularity of *St. Nicholas* can be attributed to Stockton's refusal to print anything which was written with ecclesiastical suavity —helpful, but patronizing.

That Stockton's relations with his fellow workers were kept on the same plane of amiability which so richly characterized his work is evidenced by the few details of his personal life during this period which have survived. One story reflects again his habit of naming domestic animals after his friends. Stockton was living in 1874 on a small farm in Rutherford, New Jersey.[5] Upon the arrival of a new brood of chicks, Stockton spent a pleasant afternoon naming them after his friends. One of them he named "Mary Mapes Dodge." Later, on a visit to the Stocktons, Mrs. Dodge inquired after the health of her namesake. Stockton shook his head sadly; "Imagine my surprise," he said, "when *Mary Mapes Dodge* turned out to be *Thomas Bailey Aldrich!*"

The quiet rural life, which had been a desire of Stockton's from early youth, was realized when he moved to Rutherford. While he and Mrs. Stockton were looking for a country home near New York, they had discovered a family living on a canal boat on the Harlem River. This experience was the inspiration for one of his happiest tales, "Rudder Grange," which appeared in *Scribner's Magazine* for November 1874.

"Rudder Grange" originally consisted of a single sketch telling of the adventures of Euphemia and her husband, the nameless narrator, in finding a home suited to their expensive tastes and limited income. Having written a book telling

[5] 122 Passaic Ave.

young married people how to set up their establishment,[6] Euphemia feels very competent. But she encounters difficulties because, in her book, she has put down the best quality and the lowest prices. As her husband says, "She did not mean to mislead, and her plan certainly made our book attractive. But it did not work very well in practice." [7] They determine to settle on a canal boat, and buy "just what they absolutely need, and then work up from that."

Acting on this plan, we bought first a small stove, because Euphemia said that we could sleep on the floor, if it were necessary, but we couldn't make a fire on the floor—at least not often. Then we got a table and two chairs. The next thing we purchased was hang-shelves for our books, and Euphemia suddenly remembered the kitchen things. These, which were few, with some crockery, nearly brought us to the end of our resources, but we had enough for a big easy-chair which Euphemia was determined I should have, because I really needed it when I came home at night, tired with my long day's work at the office. I had always been used to an easy-chair, and it was one of her most delightful dreams to see me in a real nice one, comfortably smoking my pipe in my own house, after eating my own delicious little supper in company with my own dear wife. We selected the chair, and then we were about to order the things sent out to our future home, when I happened to think that we had no bed. I called Euphemia's attention to the fact.

She was thunderstruck.

"I never thought of that," she said. "We shall have to give up the stove." [8]

These two, then, together with the Boarder, a young man of congenial tastes, set up their home at Rudder Grange—half-boat, half-farm.

The unusual type of hero that Stockton delighted to depict appears in "Rudder Grange." He is a self-sufficient individual, who greets the extraordinary as if it were a commonplace, and accepts frustration and disaster with imper-

6 The Home—Where It Should Be and What to Put in It. New York, 1872.
7 Rudder Grange, New York, 1887, p. 7.
8 Ibid., p. 11.

turbable serenity. Euphemia is a delightful person—and she explains many of the things that men have long wondered about women: their curious blindness, their practicality, their adaptability, their loyalty—and their eternal, unquenchable desire to improve those things which, to the discomfited male, at least, are already quite satisfactory. She is a very real person, and she emerged from the single episode of the founding of Rudder Grange as so attractive a person that it was inevitable that there should be a demand for the further chronicle of her resourcefulness. Her husband is so amiable a fellow that it is impossible to discover whether he shares naturally her characteristic of naïve simplicity, or whether he records her madhatter's logic through doting, blind love, which finds only admiration for the loved one's judgment and actions. And, if the latter is the case, a certain blindness to fault is not reprehensible in a husband, especially one who enjoys such complete reciprocal admiration and confidence as Euphemia displays for her husband on the occasion of the "burglar" at Rudder Grange:

When I reached my room I lighted the lamp, and found Euphemia still under the bed.

"Is it all right?" she asked.

"Yes," I answered, "there was no burglar. Pomona fell out the window."

"Did you get her a plaster?" asked Euphemia, drowsily.

"No, she did not need one. She's all right now. Were you worried about me, dear?"

"No, I trusted in you entirely, and I think I dozed a little under the bed." [9]

The second episode, "The Girl at Rudder Grange," [10] introduced a character destined to rival Euphemia in popularity. The girl was Pomona, the Rudder Grangers' *fille de chambre, chef de cuisine,* confidante, and maid of all work. Pomona is one of Stockton's finest portraits.

When Frank Stockton and Mary Ann Tuttle first were

9 *Ibid.,* p. 50.
10 *Scribner's Magazine,* July 1875.

married, Mary Murray, an elderly housekeeper who had been in the service of the elder Stocktons for many years, went with them to their first home in Nutley, New Jersey, because she did not wish to be separated from Frank, whom she had nursed in his infancy. Mary Murray was getting old,[11] and to help her Stockton took a young girl, Martha ———, from an orphanage which he described as "Saint Somebody's Home—a place where they keep orphans to let, so to speak." [12]

Martha's education was rudimentary and she read haltingly, but she delighted in and, despite gentle admonitions, persisted in reading that type of novel, designed for just such intellects, which retails romantically melodramatic stories of what is represented to be the English nobility. Martha read aloud, as do many persons unaccustomed to the printed word, and she experienced especial difficulty in enunciating polysyllables. She could be heard all over the house, and for a time this amused Stockton, but later it became extremely irritating. This, coupled with other circumstances, caused Mrs. Stockton to secure a position for her elsewhere.[13]

But whatever the cause of her removal may have been, Martha provided material of the particular type Stockton was able most happily to develop. Pomona of Rudder Grange became one of Stockton's permanent additions to the portrait gallery of American fiction. The same simplicity that distinguished Euphemia is found in Pomona, but in her it is allied with a natural wit, a shrewd, if untutored, sense of values, and an industrious curiosity concerning the world about her. Stockton used his material resourcefully. The Rudder Grangers' benign imbecilities seem mad enough, but none of the episodes reach the pitch of sheer fun attained when

[11] Mary Murray, a domestic, was buried in the Stockton burial plot in Woodlands Cemetery, Philadelphia, December 15, 1881. Frank Stockton's second sister, Mary Murray Stockton, was named after this old family housekeeper, attesting the affection in which she was held.

[12] *Op. cit.* p. 37.

[13] In later years Stockton declared that Martha "went on the stage and you may read her stage name in the largest of letters on a hundred posters in New York during the season." Quoted in *Author*, III: 100, 1891. But Stockton never identified her.

Pomona's literary proclivities keep Euphemia's husband toss-
ing fretfully in his bed. The scene deserves repetition.

The one thing about Pomona that troubled me more than
anything else was her taste for literature. It was not literature to
which I objected, but her very peculiar taste. She would read in
the kitchen every night after she had washed the dishes, but if
she had not read aloud it would not have made so much difference to me. But I am naturally very sensitive to external impres-
sions, and I do not like the company of people who, like our girl,
cannot read without pronouncing in a measured and distinct
voice every word of what they are reading. And when the matter
thus read appeals to one's every sentiment of aversion, and there
is no way of escaping it, the case is hard indeed.

From the first I felt inclined to order Pomona, if she could not
attain the power of silent perusal, to cease from reading altogether; but Euphemia would not hear to this.

"Poor thing!" said she, "it would be cruel to take from her
her only recreation. And she says she can't read any other way.
You needn't listen if you don't want to."

This was all very well from an abstract point of view; but the
fact was that, in practice, the more I did not want to listen, the
more I heard.

As the evenings were often cool, we sat in our dining-room,
and the partition between this room and the kitchen seemed to
have no influence whatever in arresting sound. So that when I
was trying to read or to reflect, it was by no means exhilarating
to my mind to hear from the next room that:

"The La dy Ce sel i a now si zed the weep on and all though
the boor ly vil ly an re tain ed his vy gor ous hold she drew the
blade through his fin gers and hoorl ed it far be hind her dryp
ping with jore."

This sort of thing, kept up for an hour or so at a time, used
to drive me nearly wild. But Euphemia did not mind it. I believe that she had so delicate a sense of what was proper that
she did not hear Pomona's private readings.

On one occasion even Euphemia's influence could scarcely re-
strain me from violent interference.

It was our boarder's night out, when he was detained in town
by his business, and Pomona was sitting up to let him in. This

was necessary for our front door, or main-hatchway, had no night-latch, but was fastened by means of a bolt. Euphemia and I used to sit up for him, but that was earlier in the season, when it was pleasant to be out on deck until quite a late hour. But Pomona never objected to sitting—or getting—up late, and so we allowed this weekly duty to devolve on her.

On this particular night I was very tired and sleepy, and soon after I got into bed I dropped into a delightful slumber. But it was not long before I was awakened by the fact that:

"Sa rah did not fl inch but gras ped the heat ed i ron in her un in jur ed hand and when the ra bid an i mal a proach ed she thr ust the lur id po ker in his—."

"My conscience!" said I to Euphemia, "can't that girl be stopped?"

"You wouldn't have her sit there and do nothing, would you?" said she.

"No; but she needn't read out that way."

"She can't read any other way," said Euphemia, drowsily.

"Yell af ter yell res oun ded as he wil dly spr rang—."

"I can't stand that, and I won't," said I. "Why don't she go into the kitchen,—the dining-room's no place for her."

"She must not sit there," said Euphemia. "There's a window-pane out. Can't you cover up your head?"

"I shall not be able to breathe if I do; but I suppose that's no matter," I replied.

The reading continued:

"Ha, Ha! Lord Mar mont thun der ed thou too shalt suf fer all that this poor—"

I sprang out of bed.

Euphemia thought I was going for my pistol, and she gave one bound and stuck her head out of the door.

"Pomona, fly!" she cried.

"Yes, ma'am," said Pomona; and she got up and flew—not very fast, I imagine. Where she flew to I don't know, but she took the lamp with her, and I could hear distant syllables of agony and blood, until the boarder came home and Pomona went to bed.

I think this made an impression upon Euphemia, for, although she did not speak to me upon the subject or any other, that night, the next time I heard Pomona reading, the words ran somewhat thus:

"The aston ish ing che ap ness of land is ac count ed for by the want of home mar kets, of good ro ads and che ap me ans of trans por ta tion in ma ny sec ti ons of the state." [14]

Stockton's humor frequently is based upon such episodes as this. It is one of his great charms that his humor has its source firmly in the simple details of life, but details so heightened, and presented under such circumstances, that laughter is produced effortlessly. The circus clown, an accomplished entertainer, knows that the spectacle of a high-hatted, frock-coated gentleman slipping ingloriously on a banana-peel is funny, because dignity is ludicrously lost; but he knows also that real humor is produced when the pompous gentleman, in falling, retains some fragments of his dignity by remaining unconscious of any departure from the normal. This is the humor of *Rudder Grange*.

Through the succeeding episodes of *Rudder Grange*, Stockton retains the same high standard of droll humor. When Pomona cuts a hole in the side of the scow, with the approval of Euphemia, she forgets that the tide rises, and the result is the exodus of Pomona and the establishment of the New Rudder Grange. Euphemia's new German maid, who makes a border of ham-bones around the flower bed, each hollow bone filled with earth and planted with seed; the Rudder Granger's shipment of the drunken tramp by express to the nearest police station; the purchase of the savage dog to protect Euphemia, and their rescue from the roof of the woodshed by the timely arrival of Pomona—all these episodes preserve the freshness of our first meeting with Euphemia. A note of satire creeps into "Camping Out at Rudder Grange." [15] The Rudder Grangers, upon the recommendation of a physician, get away from it all by camping on the creek a short walk from their home. Their neighbors naturally think them slightly insane. Stockton's satirical vignette of the joys of life in the woods reached near-perfection in the underpitched account of their first meal.

[14] *Rudder Grange,* pp. 39–43.
[15] *Scribner's Magazine.* May 1878.

The fire did not burn very well and while I was at work at it, Euphemia spread a cloth upon the grass, and set forth bread and butter, cheese, sardines, potted ham, preserves, biscuits, and a lot of other things.

We did not wait for the kettle to boil, but concluded to do without tea or coffee, for this meal, and content ourselves with pure water. For some reason or other, however, the creek water did not seem to be very pure, and we did not like it a bit.

"After lunch," said I, "we will go and look for a spring; that will be a good way of exploring the country."

"If we can't find one," said Euphemia, "we shall have to go to the house for water for I can never drink that stuff." [16]

The Rudder Grange stories illustrate very clearly Stockton's methods of working. Nearly all of the incidents told so amusingly in the succeeding Rudder Grange stories were based on actual happenings, and are retailed accurately, the humor arising naturally from the deft undertones in which the episodes are told. Stockton's amusing use of the book *The Home* upon which he had collaborated with Mrs. Stockton shows how easily he transmuted the commonplace into the satirically humorous. Pomona was a real girl. The Boarder, that gallant companion of the canal-boat experiment, was Mr. William H. Boardman, a lifelong friend, who boarded with the Stocktons after they settled in their second home at Rutherford, New Jersey. That he shared the Stocktons' interest in the improvement of their home, and joined wholeheartedly in their activities, is clear from the early pages of *Rudder Grange*. The chapter devoted to the Boarder's marriage and the description of his new "modern" apartment are nearly accurate representations of the actual circumstances. Euphemia's experiment in raising chickens, with her wildly astronomical expectations, is a mild satire on Stockton's own similar experiment. Euphemia calculates:

I begin with ten hens—I got four common ones, because it would make it easier to calculate. After a while, I set these ten hens on thirteen eggs each; three of these eggs will probably

16 *Ibid.*, p. 114.

spoil,—that leaves ten chickens hatched out. Of these, I will say that half die, that will make five chickens for each hen; you see, I leave a large margin for loss. This makes fifty chickens, and when we add the ten hens, we have sixty fowls at the end of the first year. Next year I set these sixty and they bring up five chickens each,—I am sure there will be a larger proportion than this, but I want to be safe,—and that is three hundred chickens; add the hens, and we have three hundred and sixty at the end of the second year. In the third year, calculating in the same way, we shall have twenty-one hundred and sixty chickens; in the fourth year there will be twelve thousand nine hundred and sixty, and at the end of the fifth year, which is as far as I need to calculate now, we shall have sixty-four thousand and eight hundred chickens. What do you think of that? At seventy-five cents apiece— a very low price,—that would be forty-eight thousand and six hundred dollars.[17]

When first established on his own small farm, Stockton had worked out a chicken-raising scheme which, he thought, would bring a handsome return. The results of course were disastrous, but he recouped his losses by selling the story of the incident for precisely the sum the chicken-raising venture had cost him. In like manner, the material of *Rudder Grange* was winnowed directly from the experiences of every day, but portrayed with such gentle satire that the reader is aware only of the humor.

As episode succeeds episode in the delightful history of Euphemia, her husband, the boarder, Pomona, and steady, indulgent Jonas, one is tempted time and again to pause and savor the happy incidents which crowd the pages. Stockton's first memorable book, episodic as it is, unplanned as it was, was the first intimation most readers had that a new, and a unique, American author was introducing into literature a new note in humor characteristically American.

Stockton has been characterized as a writer of "escapist" literature, and commentators have seen in his work a revolt against the oppressive religious atmosphere in which he lived as a youth. His reaction to an over-zealous religious régime

17 Pp. 105–106.

was simple and direct, and has already been indicated: in his mild revolt he remained a Christian, but refused to adhere to the tenets of any sect. If Stockton wrote "literature of escape," his purpose, consciously or unconsciously, was deeper than any such superficial reason, and was the result of his theory of the purpose of creative writing. He was no "realist," although he frequently made effective use of the methods of the realists; he was no "romanticist," although many of his plots are wildly romantic.[18] His method was the combination of romantic material and realistic treatment which has produced so many of the great works in our language. This method was evident in "Ting-a-ling," and as his art developed, it was the method he used in "The Lady, or the Tiger?" and in *The Casting Away of Mrs. Lecks and Mrs. Aleshine*.

But during this period of his maturing art, Stockton was experimenting with a method of treating classical, familiar material with realistic objectivity. Homely experiences from the early days of his marriage provided the material. The dispassionate, unadorned, unheroic recital of events as seen through the eyes of an apparently unimaginative narrator provided the method. It was a method that made *Rudder Grange* distinguished fiction, and one which he used frequently in tales such as "My Well and What Came Out of It"[19] and "My Unwilling Neighbor."[20]

Rudder Grange was written during the latter part of 1873 and the early months of 1874. The continuous success of succeeding stories about Euphemia and Pomona prompted Stockton to gather them into a loosely integrated book. He sent the manuscript to several publishers, each of whom returned it. Roberts Brothers, of Boston, returned it with a polite note to the effect that, as Stockton phrased it, "they felt the public pulse, and they regretted to remark that it did not beat in warm throbs for me."[21]

18 *Vide: The Great Stone of Sardis; The Great War Syndicate; The Adventures of Captain Horn; The Vizier of the Two Horned Alexander*, etc.
19 In *A Story-Teller's Pack*, New York, 1897, pp. 277–309.
20 *McClure's Magazine*, Vol. XIII (December 1896), p. 155.
21 By 1891, *Rudder Grange* had sold over 40,000 copies.

In 1874–75, while he was working on the early episodes of *Rudder Grange,* Stockton was also busy on the preparation of another juvenile book, *Tales Out of School.*[22] *Tales Out of School* followed the pattern of *Roundabout Rambles,* but its stories were more entertaining and less didactic. Where *Roundabout Rambles* was directly informative, *Tales Out of School,* while providing much information, presented its material in story form, as anecdotes, so that the little adventures in natural history (which comprise the bulk of these short pieces) became picturesque and exciting.

But the "Rudder Grange" stories and *Tales Out of School* did not interfere with Stockton's work on *St. Nicholas.* All who were associated with him here heaped unstinting praise upon his conduct of the magazine. He was, in a large measure, responsible for its success. Under his own name, and his two *noms de plume,* stories and articles directed to his juvenile audience and, he sometimes hoped, his adult audience as well, appeared in each issue. While the material varies in quality, generally it holds to a very high level of achievement for one who was a busy editor.

So intensive was his work that his eyes, never strong, and for long years subjected to severe strain, were affected to such an extent that during 1876 he was unable to read for any length of time without extreme fatigue and pain. Only one story, "America's Birthday Party," in the April issue, appeared during the year.

In search of a rest, therefore, on February 8, 1877, Mr. and Mrs. Stockton went to Painesville, Virginia, Mrs. Stockton's home. On the 18th they went to Florida, and in company with a friend, crossed to the Bahamas. They remained in the South for some weeks, and the trip was apparently most successful. Stockton's eyes improved, he was refreshed by familiar scenes in Virginia, and new scenes in Florida. It did much to provide new material. *A Jolly Fellowship* (1880) was one of the most notable results of the trip, and the beauty of Nassau and the Bahamas made so deep an impression that

22 *Tales Out of School,* New York (Scribner, Armstrong), 1875.

he wrote one of his few strictly informative travel papers, "An Isle of June." [23]

Upon his return, Stockton took up again his duties as assistant Editor of *St. Nicholas* which, during his absence, had been capably administered by William F. Clarke.[24]

A letter written to Clarke on July 7, 1877, reveals that Stockton had returned from Florida with a deflated purse—a not unusual experience following a trip to Florida even before the moon was discovered over Miami.

Philadelphia, July 7, 1877

Dear Mr. Clarke:

Here is the proof. I think I have taken out just about forty lines. Call on me freely whenever you want anything of the kind done. Good Mrs. D[odge] has gone to Cutchhhhhhhh,[25] but hope she decided on that Russian Story before she went. (I sent you a batch of electro-work the other day which I suppose you received). I would not say anything about the consideration of these, were it not that I need all the cash I can raise just at this particular juncture. By the way, that same thing has happened before to about 89642173820135 people.

Yours truly,

Frank R. Stockton

On November 3, 1877, Stockton's younger brother, John Drean Stockton, who of all his family had been closest to him, died. For a few years their paths had diverged, Frank's work taking him to New York, while John's newspaper, the *Post,* had kept him in Philadelphia. But they had been chums as boys, had studied together, had rambled in the woods together, had worked together as young men. Stockton felt his brother's death keenly.

Resumption of work brought about a return of his eye infection, and during 1878 Stockton was forced to give up his

---

[23] *Scribner's Monthly,* Vol. XV (November 1877), p. 13.

[24] William Fayle Clarke (1855–1937) joined the staff of *St. Nicholas* in 1873. He became Associate Editor in 1893, and Editor in 1905. He died August 22, 1937.

[25] *Sic.* Possibly Chimquassabumtook, or Cauquomgomoc, Maine.

work on *St. Nicholas* permanently. William F. Clarke took his place as assistant editor. For several years Stockton was unable to read or write at all, except at great intervals and for very short periods, but his retirement from *St. Nicholas* was not altogether due to his failing sight. For years he had cherished a desire to support himself wholly by free-lance writing, and now that he was finding a ready market for his stories, he took advantage of the retirement his affliction imposed, and resigned from the staff of *St. Nicholas,* although he contributed stories and sketches in considerable volume to the magazine as late as 1897. Stockton had the natural desire of any writer for a wider audience, and he made the most of the popularity of the "Rudder Grange" stories.

In 1879 he collected the stories of Euphemia and her husband, the Boarder, and Pomona, and the resulting volume, *Rudder Grange,* was published by Scribners in April. With its publication Frank Stockton took his place as a creator of American literature.

A second edition of *Rudder Grange* was soon called for, and Stockton added several new chapters. One of these was the story of Pomona's baby.[26]

Harkins' *Little Pilgrimages* records another "typical Stockton story" concerning this baby:

I had planned out a book of Pomona's travels, [Stockton said], and was about ready to write it. I was in Philadelphia at the time, and had a business appointment with my dentist, an old friend. By the way, you should never change your dentist any more than you should your plumber. Both will want to take out the work of their predecessors, swearing that it was done very badly. Well, while in the chair, I got to talking with this dentist friend about my new book. I told him, I had serious thoughts of killing the baby. He was very much interested. We talked over the advisability of doing this, and while he was not convinced, he in the main agreed with me.

I had been finished with, and clasping his hand, went into the waiting room on my way out. This waiting room was filled with

26 "The Baby at Rudder Grange," Ch. XIX, *Rudder Grange,* New York, 1887.

women. As I passed through the door I heard him call, "Then you have positively decided to kill that baby?"

"Positively," I replied.

You should have seen the women stare. It was not until I got well out in the hallway that I realized what they must, of course, have thought.[27]

During the years immediately following his retirement as assistant editor of *St. Nicholas Magazine,* Stockton was forced to be extremely careful of his eyes. Any prolonged reading or writing brought pain, and forced him to rest for several days. In order to continue his work he began to dictate his stories to his wife. For a number of years Marian Stockton served as his amanuensis, giving up her labors only when his revenues were sufficient to warrant a paid secretary. In 1878 three "Rudder Grange" stories appeared in *Scribner's Magazine,* and five short stories [28] and a serial, *A Jolly Fellowship* were printed in *St. Nicholas.*

In 1879 "Pomona's Bridal Trip," in *Scribner's,* and five articles in *St. Nicholas* gave evidence of Stockton's industry under adverse conditions. In 1880 he had three articles in the January *St. Nicholas,* one in February, two in July, one in October, one in November, and two in December, the whole representing a good year's work.[29]

An indirect result of Stockton's trip to Florida and the Bahamas was the publication in 1878 of *A Jolly Fellowship* as a serial, running from November 1878 to October 1879 in *St. Nicholas.* In 1880 Scribners published it in book form. Where *What Might Have Been Expected* had shown a power of sustained narrative in one whose usual *metier* was the short

[27] Edward F. Harkins, *Little Pilgrimages Among Men who Have Written Famous Books,* Boston, 1901, pp. 112–114.

[28] "Something in the Old Clothes Line" (January); "Huckleberry" (February); "Old Nicolai" (April); "The Emergency Mistress" (August); "Poor Relations" (November).

[29] *The Century Magazine* for July 1880 carried one of Stockton's two identifiable appearances as an artist—except, of course, for earlier work done professionally. It is entitled "The Advantages of Ballast," and exhibits graphically Stockton's chief ability as a humorist—the practical mind contemplating the extraordinary with placid assurance that everything will come out all right if the situation is met with uncommon sense.

story, *A Jolly Fellowship* blended humor, caricature, and adventure in a way which gave evidence that Stockton could write a story which had a well-articulated plot. But it gave evidence, too, of a lack which Stockton was not ever quite able to supply—an inability fully, or even picturesquely, to localize his stories. The scenes of *A Jolly Fellowship* shift rapidly, but they are scenes which, in 1878, before the exploitation of the tourist trade was worked out into its latter-day technique, must have been genuinely quaint and picturesque. Savannah, St. Augustine, and Nassau form the background against which the boyish adventures are played, but nothing of the color, the tropical richness of these places comes through the narrative.[30]

Yet Stockton loved to travel, and he was a sensitive traveler. He approached each strange city and each new country with sympathy and a desire to see them whole, in their relations to national history and characteristics. He was never the "typical American traveler," critical, fault-finding, superior. The reason he failed clearly to localize his stories, the reason he could not write vivid descriptions of his settings, seems to be that he was more immediately concerned with imaginative situations and character than he was with the place in which the action was taking place. One who reads Stockton intensively will soon realize that he seldom particularizes; geographical details generally are vague; his descriptions of imaginative machinery, as in *The Great Stone of Sardis,* seemingly detailed, actually are but skillful presentations of well-established physical principles;[31] almost never are the details of dress or appearance of his characters given. As a matter of fact, the definitely fantastic stories, such as "Ting-a-ling" or "Prince Hassak's March," and the stories of ghosts, like "The Bishop's Ghost and the Printer's Baby," are more fully documented with realistic details than is usual with any of his other work. Stockton realized clearly that the more

---

[30] Indeed, so vague is Stockton in localizing his stories that Mrs. Lecks and Mrs. Aleshine have been variously reported as being New Jersey, Pennsylvania, Middle States, and New England housewives!
[31] For a fuller discussion of this, see Chapter VI.

circumstantial his detail in the stories of fantasy, the more credible would they appear. It is the very humanness of the "Griffin" which makes his friendship for the Minor Canon believable, and gives point and force to the allegory. But Stockton was correct in assuming that, in his stories of real life, he need not localize, since character and situation were sufficient to carry his idea, however much specific location and particulars of dress and appearance might have illuminated it. *A Jolly Fellowship* is a bright juvenile narrative, and is, incidentally, one of the few long stories which he wrote definitely for an immature audience.

That he had established himself as a writer who could command good prices for his work is to be seen from a letter written to Mary Mapes Dodge concerning the price of a new serial, following *A Jolly Fellowship,* for *St. Nicholas.*

Charlottesville, Albemarle Co., Va.
October 30/80

Dear Mrs. Dodge:

I sent to the office, yesterday, the Ms. of "The Story of Viteau," the historical serial, which, to my great relief, I have just finished. While I do not want to give anyone any extra work to do (you know how my whole soul revolts at such an idea) I would be very glad to have the story decided upon, as soon as convenient, being desirous to "realize" thereupon. The Ms. you remember, was to be submitted as a whole, and not in installments.

We have said nothing about the price of the story. Of course, it is harder to write a complete serial of six parts, than the half of one of twelve parts, but whether or not I am paid more than half the sum I received for my last serial ["A Jolly Fellowship"] ($1500) will depend entirely upon you and the publishers.

I have tried to make the story reflect the peculiar spirit and customs of the time (the early part of the thirteenth century) and to give a natural picture of the life of the boys and girls of the Middle Ages. I have endeavored also to avoid the stilted and unnatural style of conversation seen in many historical novels, and have given as much characteristic action and incident as possible. Each installment is divided into three chapters, to vary the scene and action.

I hope to hear that you like the story, and am, always,

Yours very truly

Frank R. Stockton

Mrs. Dodge has written upon the letter, "I said worth $850 at least." This was perhaps the last time that Stockton permitted the publisher to determine the price he should pay. For a short article in *St. Nicholas* he was receiving $100, and he had something in nearly every issue. Later, he was asking, and receiving, $150 a story from *St. Nicholas* and a minimum of $300 for contributions to other magazines.

His trip to Florida did more for Stockton, however, than provide him with material for stories. His health had been so seriously affected that it became imperative for him to give up his writing, for a time, entirely. In March 1880, with Mrs. Stockton and three friends, he returned to Florida for an extensive stay. A description of this trip in a letter to Mrs. Dodge gives an unusually vivid, if somewhat oblique, picture of him at this period. His remarks on the future "Euphemia Among the Pelicans," and on the proposed change in *Scribner's Magazine,* have an especial interest.

Charlottesville, Va.

May 19, 1881

Dear Mrs. Dodge,

You must not be surprised at receiving another dictated letter. I am not-at-all sure that I could not write this one without injury to my various faculties, but the rest from writing has been so advantageous that I have determined to keep it up, at least, till next Fall. Besides I have become so accustomed to being a Dictator and to writing "per-M"-torily, that I have grown to like it.

I want to tell you of the very pleasant trip we had down the Lodian river. I will not insult you by telling you in what part of Florida the Lodian river is, but I have been obliged to inform nearly every other person of my acquaintance, to whom I spoke on the subject, that it is a long arm of the sea running down the east coast of Florida, and separated from the ocean by a narrow strip of land—sometimes not over a hundred yards wide. The river varies in width from six miles to thirty yards. Great-portions of its shores are entirely unsettled and much of its scenery, is wild and novel.

When I determined to take my holiday last March, Mrs. Stockton and I, with three young friends, a lady and two gentlemen, went up the St. John's river, nearly its entire length, a very picturesque and interesting trip; and then proceeded overland to Titusville on the Lodian River. There we chartered a sail boat for our journey to Jupiter Inlet, the southern limit of the river. The boat was the largest we could get, but was not large enough to accommodate the whole party at night, so we took with us a tent. Our entire trip occupied three weeks, during which Mrs. Stockton and I slept on that boat. We were six days going down the river, stopping every night to camp. At St. Jupiter Inlet we made a permanent camp, where we staid ten days; putting up the tent, a rude palmetto hut, and permanently mooring the boat. I saved you a view of the boat, and one of the camp, which were taken by the assistant keeper of Jupiter light-house, who had a camera. We were within half a mile of the ocean; and the river at that place, is one of the finest fishing grounds on the continent. We fished two or three times every day, and had splendid sport. We caught, altogether over seven hundred pounds of fish,—many of the fish being very large. The finest, principally blue-fish and bass, we picked out for our own eating, and gave the rest to a man at the light-house who was salting fish for the market. The light-house was about a mile from our camp, across the river, and was the only habitation within twenty or thirty miles of us. Our style of living was very primitive, but we laid in a good stock of provisions at Titusville, and enjoyed our life exceedingly. Our boatman was a good cook, and his little boy was general assistant, and handed round the cups, and dishes. For the whole of the three weeks we lived almost entirely in the open air, (the cabin of the boat being open at one end) and yet none of us took cold, and all thrived exceedingly. The water of the river was salt, making its influence perfectly healthful, and we had fine weather during the whole trip, being visited by two short gales only.

There were more interesting incidents that I won't bore you

with now, but you can imagine what a delightful time we had. Some of the scenery on the river, especially in "the Narrows," was wonderfully tropical, and beautiful. On our return trip we stopped at a little solitary store to replenish part of our stock of provisions, and our boatman told us we had better get here all that we wanted, for it was sixty-five miles to the next store. This will give you an idea of how much the country is "opened up."

When we finished our charming journey, we regretfully gave up our open-air-life, and returned to the habits of civilization.

This reads, my dear Mrs. Dodge like an article for a magazine, but it is, indeed a friendly letter. I knew that you and Mr. Clarke will take an interest in our wanderings. I expect to make a Rudder Grange paper of the trip.

I have been greatly interested, of course, in the recent changes in the Scribner firm. I think these changes will be of great advantage to the magazines. It will seem strange at first to call our old Scribner's Monthly, "The Century", but we will get used to it in time; and there will be no mistakes and misconceptions on the part of the public in regard to the new firm.

I hope that your health will improve as the fine days of summer come on. So far it must have been, this spring, both too hot, and too cool in New York. Here, we are now sitting before an open wood fire. I expect to spend the summer here, to work moderately, and to get myself into as good a condition as possible by Fall, when I hope to see you.

> With best love from
> Mrs. Stockton, and myself,
> Yours very truly
> Frank R. Stockton

In 1881 Stockton published one of his finest collections of fairy tales, *The Floating Prince*. As with all his fairy tales— or, as he preferred to call them, fanciful tales—the book was issued ostensibly for children. Actually he intended it for maturest readers. The tales which compose *The Floating Prince* originally appeared in *St. Nicholas*, but Stockton wanted them to have the permanence which publication between boards brings.

It would be difficult to be too enthusiastic about *The Float ing Prince.* Stockton's finest fancy, his most delicate satire, and his most wise "little truths," went into the writing of the ten stories of which the volume is composed. Not all the stories are of even merit, but at least five of them—"The Floating Prince," "How the Aristocrats Sailed Away," "The Reformed Pirate," "The Gudra's Daughter," and "The Magician's Daughter and the High-Born Boy"—are among the finest of their kind. Their charm is fragile, depending chiefly upon that deft mixture of the normal and the incongruous at which Stockton was so capable. Who but Stockton could soberly narrate the tale of the way in which the Floating Prince acquired his kingdom?

If I want a kingdom, I must build up one for myself, and that is just what I will do. I will gather together my subjects as I go along. The first person I meet shall be my chief councilor of state, the second shall be head of the army, and the third shall be admiral of the navy, the next shall be chief treasurer, and then I will collect subjects of various classes.

The Prince meets first, and takes into his service, a fairy as chief councilor ("I know a good deal about government. I have been governed ever so much and I could not help learning how it is done.") He meets a giant, who becomes head of the army, a shepherd on stilts, who becomes admiral of the navy, a clam-digger who becomes chancellor of the exchequer since he muses optimistically, "it might, in the end, be better than clam-digging." Next, the Prince and his ministers surround and capture a school, impressing the classes in Compound Fractions and Long Division into service as aristocrats. For common people, the rapidly increasing if somewhat peripatetic kingdom acquires a caravan composed of men of high degree, of philosophers and rich merchants. The fairy-privy-councilor provides, by magical means, a beautiful city, into which it is deemed imprudent to introduce the aristocrats.

"I'm really sorry for those poor aristocrats, but it will never do to take them to the royal city. They are not needed, and they would make all sorts of trouble. There is nothing to be done but to let the admiral sail away with them. . . ."

"How the Aristocrats Sailed Away" tells the merry story of a school in revolt. The aristocrats capture the schoolmaster and the four philosophers who have been detailed to supervise their training. Bags are put over their heads, and their hands and feet are bound. The ship docks at a strange, silent city. The aristocrats, in attempting to ascend a magnificent staircase, find themselves on a treadmill which winds up the city like a mechanical toy, and permits it to resume activity for ten years, when it will run down again. In their adventures, they incur the displeasure of the king, from whom they escape by taking refuge in the public library, "which was closed very early every evening and opened very late every morning." To supply food, they decide by lot to become letter carriers, and every day for nine years they distribute manuscripts from the archives of the library to everyone in the city. The citizens thus "gradually become better and better educated."

In the meantime the schoolmaster and the philosophers, through the good offices of the cook, have managed to escape. Stockton gives a hilariously satirical picture of the thinker who is not prepared to act.

"Now, then," said the admiral the next day, as he sat with the helm in his hand, "we are free again to sail where we please— But I do not like to sail without an object. What shall be our object?"

The philosophers immediately declared that nothing could be more proper than that they should take a voyage to make some great scientific discovery.

"All right," said the admiral. "That suits me. What discovery shall we make?"

The philosophers were not prepared to answer this question at that moment, but they said they would try to think of some good discovery to make.

So the philosophers sat in a row behind the admiral, and thought and thought; and the admiral sat at the helm, with his blue-and-red stilts dangling in the water behind; and the cook prepared the meals, swept the deck, dusted the sail, and put things in order.

After several hours, the admiral turned around to ask the philosophers if they had thought of any discovery yet, when, to his amazement, he saw that each one of them had put his bag upon his head.

"What did you do that for?" cried the admiral, when each of the philosophers gave a little start; and then they explained that it was much easier to think with one's head in a bag. The outer world was shut out, and trains of thought were not so likely to be broken up.

So, for day after day, the philosophers, with their heads in their bags, sat, and thought, and thought; and the admiral sat and stared, and the navy cooked and dusted and kept things clean.

Matters end happily, of course. After eleven years of sailing and thinking the philosophers return to the mechanical city; the schoolboys are now grown men, and the king is delighted to receive their suggestion that he wind up his own city when it begins to run down.

Here, as in *Rudder Grange,* the humor and the charm of the stories lie in the fact that commonplace people do extraordinary things, matter-of-factly, and extraordinary people are blandly unaware of anything uncommon in their appearance or their conduct.

"The Reformed Pirate" is a study in human perspective. Meeting Carette, a little girl of adventurous disposition, the Reformed Pirate, who knits "tidies" as penance for his former career of crime on the high seas, agrees to visit a practising wizard who will reduce them to a size suitable for paying a visit to two friendly but diminutive fairies. The purpose is achieved, and the Pirate pockets the magic "little pink ball" which reduces the size of anything upon which it is placed.

Reduced in size, Carette and the Pirate are disappointed to discover that the fairies are no bigger than they themselves, and have, therefore, lost their novelty. By means of the pink ball, he reduces the fairies, and their home to a size (one-quarter inch) proportionate to their former normal relationship. But upon their return to their homes, Carette and the Pirate discover that they are permanently diminutive themselves, whereupon the Pirate climbs laboriously to the top of the church steeple, places the pink ball thereon, and reduces the entire town and its citizenry to his own size. "In the whole country there were only two persons, Carette and the Pirate, who really believed that they were condensed."

"The Gudra's Daughter" was a similar study in the proportions of human relations and human endeavor. It brings into prominence the giant dwarf, the dwarf giant, and the ordinary man, who are all the same height. The Gudra's daughter learns "that the largest dwarf is no bigger than the smallest giant, and that neither of them is larger than an ordinary man." The Stocktonian moral is characteristic.

"The Magician's Daughter and the High-Born Boy" presents the notion that the obvious solution to a problem is probably the right one. "Huckleberry" presents the idea that people ask questions mainly in order to give their own solutions. "The Emergency Mistress" asks the question "Satan himself has got me in his power—how can I ever get away from him?" To which a sensible gnome answers, "Let go of his tail!" "The Sprig of Holly" applauds one who, for temporary value, refuses to barter permanent servitude. "Derido, or the Giant's Quilt" is another lesson in Stocktonian proportion, and "The Castle of Bim" expresses the notion that "we have all thought of some place where everything shall be just as we want it to be, but I don't believe any of us will find that place."

The stories in *The Floating Prince* are by no means the moral capsules the above résumé would indicate them to be. The fairy tales of Oscar Wilde are remembered for their color and their simplicity; but the stories of Stockton are memorable for more important reasons. They are, in so far as they were written for children, mature; they are, in so far as they were written for mature minds, of deceptive simplicity. Their flavor is elusive, their charm dependent upon the attitude of the reader. It was Stockton's desire that they should be "discovered" by adults, and be accepted for what they are —shrewd commentaries on human nature and human blindness.

The publication of *The Floating Prince* was an event with which Stockton was particularly pleased, because it afforded an opportunity to gain the attention of that wider audience for whom his stories were really written. He was forced to publish them in *St. Nicholas,* for no other periodical would print—or pay—for them. But as his work progressed, it becomes more and more evident that his stories were intended primarily for the critical appreciation of adults. As one whose living depended on his pen, Stockton still took advantage of the lucrative juvenile market he had established, but even his so-called fantasies were aimed only ostensibly at this audience. Actually, they were for the delectation of those who had eyes to see; who were mature enough to realize that Stockton was picturing life in terms of faëry only because he could not otherwise express his little truths. He was a conscientious realist who preferred to speak in allegory and parable.

In 1881 it was twenty-six years since Stockton had published his first story in *The American Courier.* In that time he had reached a position in which he had an assured income from writing. He was known to the editors of many magazines; he had a select audience; he had found definite markets for his work; and he had published eight books—one of which, *Rudder Grange,* had brought him a reputation as a humorist.

Twenty years of life—and his best work—were before him. The story of a happy life which had begun in 1860 was entering a period of ripe development, of success, of admiration, and of contentment. If it was a placid life Stockton led, yet it was one rich in friendship, good work, and serene living. Few men have been so blessed.

Chapter V

A DULL, scantily motivated love story, "In the Southeast Bastion," [1] published in January 1882, introduced a year of Stockton's career as a writer that was to produce an extraordinary effect on his work—that was, as a matter of fact, nearly to wreck the security and the position he had so hardly won in twenty-seven industrious years. But it introduced, too, the most fruitful decade of his long writing career.

In addition to six articles in *St. Nicholas Magazine* during the year, he published a short story in *The Century Magazine* which revealed a power to treat the supernatural in familiar terms which his work hitherto had but scarcely indicated. [2] The story was "The Transferred Ghost," [3] a delirious tale of a haunted ghost. Stockton's technique of giving a quite human outlook and human sympathies to fairies, gnomes, afrits, and assorted mythological monsters, while at the same time endowing them with the full equipment of their supernatural abilities, was a method so effective that he created an entire gallery of quasi-supernatural creatures. They are quite human, usually amiable. They are never frightening, and if they are sometimes gauzily immaterial, there is about them the comfortable plaintiveness of humanity which immediately arouses the sympathy of anyone who meets them.

"The Transferred Ghost" is a love story in which the narrator is visited late at night, in accordance with established ghostly custom, by the ghost of John Hinckman, who is, distressingly, not yet dead. The ghost can be heard only by the person to whom he is speaking, and a midnight conversation

1 *Harper's Monthly*, Vol. LXIV (January 1882), 278–285.
2 "The Fairy and the Ghost," *Lippincott's*, Vol. V (January 1870), p. 33., and "Cooking a Ghost," *Hearth and Home*, Vol. V, April 19, 1873.
3 *Century*, Vol. XXIV (May 1882), p. 43.

ensues, in which the ghost tells his amazed but unhorrified
listener of his sad plight. But first, the ghost reassures himself that John Hinckman, his ghostee, as it were, is out of
the house.

"Then I will go on," said the ghost, "for I am glad to have the
opportunity of talking to someone who will listen to me; but if
John Hinckman should come and catch me here, I should be
frightened out of my wits."

"This is all very strange," I said, greatly puzzled by what I
had heard. "Are you the ghost of Mr. Hinckman?"

This was a bold question, but my mind was so full of other
emotions that there seemed to be no room for that of fear.

"Yes, I am his ghost," my companion replied, "and yet I have
no right to be. And this is what makes me so uneasy; and so much
afraid of him. It is a strange story and I truly believe, without
precedent. Two years and a half ago, John Hinckman was dan-
gerously ill in this very room. At one time he was so far gone that
he was really believed to be dead. It was in consequence of too
precipitate a report in regard to this matter that I was, at the
time, appointed to be his ghost. Imagine my surprise and horror,
sir, when, after I had accepted the position and assumed its re-
sponsibilities, that old man revived, became convalescent, and
eventually regained his usual health. My situation was now one
of extreme delicacy and embarrassment. I had no power to return to my original unembodiment, and I had no right to be the
ghost of a man who was not dead. I was advised by my friends
to quietly maintain my position, and was assured that, as John
Hinckman was an elderly man, it could not be long before I
could rightfully assume the position for which I had been selected. But I tell you, sir," he continued with animation, "the
old man seems as vigorous as ever, and I have no idea how much
longer this annoying state of things will continue. I spend my
time trying to get out of that old man's way. I must not leave
this house, and he seems to follow me everywhere. I tell you,
sir, he haunts me."

The transferred ghost learns of the narrator's love for
Hinckman's niece, Madeline, and, heard only by the lover,
endeavors to aid their cause. Madeline, hearing her tortured

lover make certain testy remarks to the well-meaning but awkward ghost, supposes they are meant for her. Love matters are at sixes and sevens, and only after perspiring explanations is the narrator again in Madeline's good graces. He is about to tell Madeline he loves her, when the ghost "bursts" into the room.

"Do you know," he cried, "that John Hinckman is coming up the hill? He will be here in fifteen minutes, and if you are doing anything in the way of love-making, you had better hurry it up. But this is not what I came to tell you. I have glorious news! At last I am transferred. . . . You can't imagine how glad I am to be, at last, the real ghost of somebody."

"Oh!" I cried, rising to my feet and stretching out my arms in utter wretchedness, "I would to heaven you were mine!"

"I *am* yours," said Madeline, raising to me her tearful eyes.

In "The Transferred Ghost," and in other ghost stories, Stockton made effective use of a device which some writers of memorable stories of the supernatural have used. Of the four senses—sight, hearing, smell, and touch—which ordinarily detect the presence of a person, one, two, or three are removed. In "The Transferred Ghost," the narrator is able to see and to hear the ghost, but Madeline can neither see, hear, smell, nor touch him. This situation creates humor, but the same absence of the ordinary methods of perception can also create horror and terror, as in F. Marion Crawford's "The Upper Berth" (1894), in which sight is removed, and smell is heightened. Stockton's ghosts are always amiable; frequently they require a mere mortal to extricate them from their predicaments; and this calm alteration of the usual formula gives that freshness and novelty in which Stockton's stories were rich.

The last two decades of Frank Stockton's life were successful and happy. But, paradoxically, that success and that happiness were nearly turned to disaster by the tremendous popularity of a story which he called "In the King's Arena." It was a story written originally to be read at a party given by Mr. and Mrs. William H. Boardman, his friends in Nutley.

The punch bowl, however, provided such an atmosphere of gaiety that Stockton felt his contribution to the evening's fun was unnecessary. Later he elaborated the story, and sent it to the new *Century Magazine*.[4] Somewhat dubiously, but relying on Stockton's reputation to carry the story, the editors of the *Century* accepted it in July 1882, paying Stockton fifty dollars for it. For Stockton a long-planned trip to Europe was about to become a reality, and in the autumn of 1882 the Stocktons sailed for Queenstown and London.

William Carey, on the editorial staff of the *Century*, cabled Stockton for permission to change the title of the story from the commonplace "In the King's Arena," to "The Lady, or the Tiger?"[5] Stockton was never touchy about changes in his stories or their titles, and gave his permission. The story retitled "The Lady, or the Tiger?" was printed in the November issue of the *Century*. Slowly at first, then with rapid acceleration, notices of the strange dilemma proposed by the story began to appear in newspapers and critical reviews. "The Lady, or the Tiger?" became a sensation. In drawing rooms, in literary clubs, in salons, around the family hearth, the problem was pondered.

The essence of the popularity of "The Lady, or the Tiger?" lay solely in the unanswered, perhaps unanswerable, human problem which Stockton propounded. In a semi-barbaric kingdom, in an unspecified olden time, a monarch of quixotic humor tries offenders against the royal dignity, or against the law, by chance. In a great arena, behind different doors through which no sound can travel, are placed a beautiful woman and a ferocious tiger. The offender is thrust alone into the arena, and permitted to choose which door he shall

[4] In 1881 *Scribner's Monthly Magazine* became the present *Century.*

[5] Stockton had but little sense of the dramatic. When his titles were not obvious (e. g., "Ting-a-ling," *Rudder Grange,* "The Buller-Podington Compact"), he used the same method of selecting the obvious title in stories whose interest would have been enhanced by a more dramatic title (e. g., "A Tale of Negative Gravity," "My Bull-Calf," "A Piece of Red Calico"). But, curiously, this very inability to choose a dramatic title resulted in some of the most striking titles in American literature (e. g., "The Transferred Ghost," "Come in, New Year!" "The Bishop's Ghost and the Printer's Baby," "The Griffin and the Minor Canon," *The Casting Away of Mrs. Lecks and Mrs. Aleshine.*)

open. If, happily, the accused man chooses the door behind which the beautiful girl is concealed, then, amid pomp and flowery circumstance, he is promptly married to her, to the accompaniment of the cheers of the multitude. If, however, he opens the door behind which the tiger chafes, his execution is immediate, and the king's dignity is avenged.

In such an unhappy court a personable young member of the king's retinue was tried because he had had the impudence to fall in love with the king's beautiful but impulsive daughter. Since he was not of noble blood, there could be no question of marriage. But the princess loved the helpless young courtier, and by methods which are open only to princesses, she obtained the secret of the doors. The young lover, who was not as ignorant of the ways of maids as he appeared, knew that she would discover behind which door was the lady, and behind which door was the tiger. As he made the traditional salute to the king, who was seated in the royal box, the youth looked quickly to the princess for the signal he knew she would give. The princess motioned toward the right. Without hesitation, he turned, walked briskly across the arena, and opened the door on the right.

At this anxious moment the story ends. Stockton appends an epilogue which explains the dilemma which the princess had had to solve before she gave her signal. It is this epilogue which raises the story above the level of the "trick," and invests it with the dignity of an exposition of human strength and human frailty. It is in this epilogue that the conflicting fundamental motives of love and hate and self-preservation are given full play. The exposition is fair; the solution is left to the reader: The young lover opens the door on the right.

Now [Stockton says], the point of the story is this: Did the tiger come out of that door, or did the lady?

The more we reflect upon this question, the harder it is to answer. It involves a study of the human heart which leads us through devious mazes of passion, out of which it is difficult to find our way. Think of it, fair reader, not as if the decision of the question depended upon yourself, but upon that hot-blooded, semi-barbaric princess, her soul at a white heat beneath the combined fires of despair and jealousy. She had lost him, but who should have him!

How often, in her waking hours and in her dreams, had she started in wild horror and covered her face with her hands as she thought of her lover opening the door on the other side of which waited the cruel fangs of the tiger!

But how much oftener had she seen him at the other door! How in her grievous reveries had she gnashed her teeth and torn her hair when she saw his start of rapturous delight as he opened the door of the lady! How her soul had burned in agony when she had seen him rush to meet that woman, with her flushing cheek and sparkling eye of triumph; when she had seen him lead her forth, his whole frame kindled with the joy of recovered life; when she had heard the glad shouts from the multitude, and the wild ringing of the happy bells; when she had seen the priest, with his joyous followers, advance to the couple, and make them man and wife before her very eyes; and when she had seen them walk away together upon their path of flowers, followed by the tremendous shouts of the hilarious multitude, in which her one despairing shriek was lost and drowned!

Would it not be better for him to die at once, and go to wait for her in the blessed regions of semi-barbaric futurity?

And yet, that awful tiger, those shrieks, that blood!

Her decision had been indicated in an instant, but it had been made after days and nights of anguished deliberation. She had known she would be asked, she had decided what she would answer, and, without the slightest hesitation, she had moved her hand to the right.

The question of her decision is one not to be lightly considered, and it is not for me to presume to set myself up as the one person able to answer it. And so I leave it with all of you: Which came out of the open door—the lady or the tiger?

The problem of "The Lady, or the Tiger?" as Stockton presented it, was so fundamentally human, so fine a representation of universal emotions and conflicting human desires that it was everywhere discussed. So many thousands of letters poured in to him demanding, begging the answer, that Stockton, who at first had stubbornly refused to give any answer,

was forced to make a statement. His reply was no more satisfactory. He said, "If you decide which it was—the lady, or the
tiger—you find out what kind of a person you are yourself." It
is obvious that Stockton was wise in refusing to give his own
solution to the problem, but, consciously or unconsciously, he
seems to have given his solution—the tiger—in the story itself.
In describing the princess, Stockton writes:

This semi-barbaric king had a daughter as blooming as his most
florid fancies, and with a soul as *fervent and imperious* as his
own.—This royal maiden was well satisfied with her lover, for he
was handsome and brave to a degree unsurpassed in all this kingdom, and she *loved him with an ardor that had enough of bar-
barism in it to make it exceedingly warm and strong.*[6]

Stockton pictures an *imperious, semi-barbaric* princess who
is in love with a brave man, but who is *not* convinced that her
love is fully returned.

How in her grievous reveries had she gnashed her teeth and
torn her hair when she saw his start of *rapturous delight* as he
opened the door of the lady.
She had lost him, but who should have him?

[The lady] was one of the fairest and loveliest of the damsels
of the Court . . . and the princess hated her. Often she had seen,
or imagined she had seen, this fair creature throwing glances of
admiration upon the person of her lover, and sometimes she
thought these glances were perceived and even returned.
She had lost him, but who should have him?

The sentence seems to be the unconscious revelation of
Stockton's own belief.[7] The same notion in favor of the tiger

[6] *Italics mine.*

[7] This hypothesis that Stockton himself, consciously or unconsciously, favored the tiger is not mere wishful thinking, nor is it a marshaling of evidence
to prove a predetermined conclusion. (1) Stockton was a logician (cf. p. 10)
and his argument in favor of the tiger (see above) is the more logical. (2) His
usual practice was to elaborate a character or a situation with full circumstantial detail (cf. p. 46); he does not do this for those elements which favor
the lady. (3) His usual practice was to print a story without revising the first
draught, yet he revised the ending of "The Lady, or the Tiger?" five times—
obviously in an attempt to balance the arguments for the lady with those

was expressed by Robert Browning when the problem was presented to him. He replied:

According to your desire I read the story in question last evening, and have no hesitation in supposing that such a princess, under such circumstances would direct her lover to the tiger's door; mind, I emphasize *such* and *so* circumstanced a person.[8]

It is, however, the sheer human interest of the problem that Stockton proposed which gives "The Lady, or the Tiger?" its valid claim as one of the world's great short stories.[9]

On May 7, 1888, *The Lady or the Tiger?*, a three-act operetta, was produced at Wallack's Theatre, New York. The run of the play was comparatively short, but it served to enhance further the reputation of Frank Stockton. The opening night was "brilliant"; Mr. and Mrs. Stockton, together with Mary Mapes Dodge and a group of friends attended; but the slightness of the plot, to which Stockton's story had contributed only the title and the central idea, combined with uninspired music, was not sufficient to make the operetta a success. De Wolf Hopper played the part of the king, and reviews of the performance praise his barbaric portrayal, commenting particularly on the felicitous repetition of the phrase, "I'm just as just as Aristides!" in that booming voice which is still well remembered. So successful was the operetta expected to be that another company opened in London, at the Elephant and Castle Theatre, on the same night, May 7, 1888. The London production fared no better than the American production, although the latter was revived for a short run a few years later.

In 1885 Stockton replied to the deluge of requests, petitions, entreaties, and demands for a solution to the riddle of

for the tiger. The argument for the choice of the tiger is inherently, as well as dramatically, the stronger; therefore, the reason for the several revisions was to bolster the weaker side.

[8] "How I Wrote 'The Lady, or the Tiger?' and What Came of the Writing of It," *Ladies' Home Journal*, November 1893, pp. 1–2.

[9] For a detailed discussion of the widespread, perennial interest in "The Lady, or the Tiger?" see "The Lady, the Tiger, and the Author," by Walter L. Pforzheimer, *Colophon*, New Series, Vol. I, Number 2, pp. 261–270.

"The Lady, or the Tiger?" by writing "The Discourager of Hesitancy." [10] "The Discourager of Hesitancy" is in many ways as ingenious a problem as "The Lady, or the Tiger?" and in some ways it is a better story. As the young lover in "The Lady, or the Tiger?" was about to open the door in the arena, a stranger witnessing the scene was unable to bear the suspense, and, rushing from the arena, he left the city. His story, when told in his native city, so interested the inhabitants that a delegation was appointed to visit the king and ask "Which came out of the door—the lady, or the tiger?" On their arrival, they are greeted courteously, and the king tells them a story: A handsome prince, seeking a bride and learning that the most beautiful damsels were assembled in the king's court, comes to ask for a wife. The king's ever delicate dignity was, as usual, affronted, but he complied with the prince's request in a characteristic manner. The prince was prepared for his wedding in barbaric splendor, but close to his side a gigantic slave, the Discourager of Hesitancy, carelessly flourished a razor-sharp scimitar. At the ceremony, the prince was blindfolded. He knew only that he was being married to a very beautiful woman. When the blindfold was ripped from his eyes, he saw a line of forty beautiful women from which he was commanded to select his bride. Should he choose the right one, he would be permitted to depart with her in peace. Should he fail—! The Discourager of Hesitancy is uncomfortably importunate. As he walks hopefully along the line of beautiful women, one frowns, one smiles. At the very last moment, as the Discourager is raising the scimitar, the prince chooses—correctly. The delegation is assured that if they decide which of the two—the damsel who frowned, or the damsel who smiled—the prince correctly judged to be his wife, they will be told which came out of the door, the lady, or the tiger.

The edge of interest in the problem was, of course, blunted by its similarity to "The Lady, or the Tiger?" but "The Discourager of Hesitancy" is of itself a good story. The Discourager, with his everlasting "I am here!" is a worthy Stocktonian

[10] *Century,* Vol. XXX (July 1885), p. 482.

concept. It is interesting, too, to note that "The Discourager of Hesitancy" changes the stress upon the central situation. In the first story there is a clear choice between love and jealousy, between self-sacrifice and a fierce possessiveness. In the second story the motive resolves into a simple matter of male vanity—did the one girl frown because she was disappointed? Did the other smile because she was pleased with her husband? This is a difficult question for any personable young man to resolve at any time, but the more particularly difficult when a nervous scimitar is limiting the time for meditation.

While the literary furore caused by the publication of "The Lady, or the Tiger?" was raging, Mr. and Mrs. Stockton were placidly touring Europe, unaware of the crisis in Stockton's writing career which the phenomenal success of the story was to precipitate. Stockton was pleased with the interest in his work aroused by the problem story, and he sought, naturally, to capitalize it. But he began to receive apologetic letters of rejection from editors to whom he had sent stories, usually at their own request. The letters expressed regret that the stories were not quite up to the standard or the quality to be expected from the author of such a magnificent tale as "The Lady, or the Tiger?". Why didn't Stockton send his best?

Stockton came perilously close to being tagged permanently as "the man who had written one great story." Only his established audience, who remembered *Rudder Grange, The Floating Prince,* and "The Transferred Ghost" enabled him to command again the attention of editors for his run-of-the-mill stories, however high their quality. "His Wife's Deceased Sister" [11] is an autobiographical tale depicting the difficulties Stockton had for a time in placing his stories. His opening is revelatory.

When I was quite a young man I adopted literature as a profession, and having passed through the necessary preparatory grades, I found myself, after a good many years of hard and often unremunerative work, in possession of what might be called a

11 *Century,* Vol. XXVII (January 1884), p. 463.

fair literary practice. My articles, grave, gay, practical, or fanciful, had come to be considered with a favor by the editors of the various periodicals for which I wrote, on which I found in time I could rely with a very comfortable certainty. My productions created no enthusiasm in the reading public; they gave me no great reputation or very valuable pecuniary return; but they were always accepted, and my receipts from them, at the time to which I have referred, were regular and reliable as a salary, and quite sufficient to give me more than a comfortable support.

The narrator tells of the writing of a story, "His Wife's Deceased Sister," inspired by the first ecstasy of his marriage. He tells of its success, and of his hopes for permanent literary recognition. And he tells of the successive rejections which his new stories receive. Ruin faces him, a disaster which he avoids only by perseverance and his own essential skill. Slowly, painfully, he rebuilds his career. The birth of a son inspires another story—as good as, if not better than, "His Wife's Deceased Sister."

"Be strong and firm," [his wife tells him]. "A great danger threatens us but you must brace yourself against it. Be strong and firm."

I pressed her hand, and we said no more that night.

The next day I took the manuscript I had just written, and carefully infolded it in stout wrapping paper. Then I went to a neighboring grocery store and bought a small, strong tin box, originally intended for biscuit, with a cover that fitted tightly. In this I placed my manuscript, and then I took the box to a tinsmith and had the top fastened on it with hard solder. When I went home I ascended into the garret and brought down to my study a ship's cash box, which had once belonged to one of my family who was a sea-captain. This box was very heavy, and firmly bound with iron, and was secured by two massive locks. Calling my wife, I told her of the contents of the tin case, which I then placed in the box, and having shut down the heavy lid, I doubly locked it.

"This key," said I, putting it in my pocket, "I shall throw into the river when I go out this afternoon."

The difficulty of living up to the standard set by "The Lady, or the Tiger?" was discussed by Stockton in a frank letter written to his old friend, George Cary Eggleston:

> After I had written that story, all the editors of all the periodicals wrote asking me to furnish them with short stories. Of course I had a quiver full, and, as these people seemed anxious for them, I thought that my harvest had come. So I proceeded to write with all my might. But presently the stories began coming back to me with editorial regrets that they did not seem to be equal to "The Lady, or the Tiger?". In other words, I found that I had ruined my own market by furnishing one story which I could not quite live up to. I succeeded after a while in selling the rejected stories here, there, and everywhere, but this experience was annoying. Among the rejected stories were "Plain Fishing," "The Reversible Landscape" and others.
>
> I wrote "His Wife's Deceased Sister" in the bitterness of my soul at that period, as a protest against the assumption that when a man does his very best he places himself under obligation to do as well on every succeeding occasion or starve to death for lack of ability to do so.[12]

Stockton's method of capitalizing on experience is clearly demonstrated by "His Wife's Deceased Sister." But of the situation created by "The Lady, or the Tiger?" Stockton was temporarily ignorant. Late in 1882 the Stocktons had gone to Europe, and they did not return until June 29, 1884—a year and a half later. Mr. Stockton was in poor health, but the sea trip, and the novelty of travel in Europe, enabled him to enjoy himself. Calais, Paris (for a long stay), Avignon, were each in turn explored. Since his failing sight prevented him from either reading or writing, Mrs. Stockton kept a detailed journal in which they recorded each day's experiences. Stockton now applied to the absorption of scenes in the Old World the same painstaking quality that he brought to the construction of his stories. Rome was studied thoroughly—the Vatican, St. Peter's, the Colosseum, by day and by moonlight, San Clemente, The Tomb of Hadrian, the Catacombs, the Cam-

---

[12] Quoted by Edwin W. Bowen in *Sewanee Review*, Vol. XI, pp. 476–477.

pagna, the palaces of the Caesars—all that was to be seen in the Eternal City was seen.

Sorrento and Capri and the Blue Grotto were visited, as were Naples, Genoa, Pisa, Florence, and Venice. In Venice he was ill for a time during June 1883. Upon recovery, so slow it made him temporarily semi-invalid, the Stocktons went north to Switzerland, where they ascended the Rigi and sailed on the Lake of Lucerne. Then, in whirlwind fashion, they toured Holland—Rotterdam and Amsterdam—Germany, with stop-offs at Cologne and Coblentz, and thence on to Belgium and Antwerp. Nearing their long trip's end, they went back to Paris for another stay before the trip across the Channel to Dover and London, on April 18, 1884. The remainder of their time abroad, until mid-June, was spent in England, chiefly in the rural counties. They visited the Stockton homestead in Malpas Parish, toured the cathedral cities in the north of England, where Chester Cathedral provided the inspiration for "The Griffin and the Minor Canon," stopped at country inns when their interest in the genuinely quaint was aroused. London provided an untiring succession of sights and sounds, many of which later become Pomona's own experiences abroad. The tomb of Chaucer in Westminster Abbey stirred Stockton's imagination—a stirring which resulted felicitously in "The Bishop's Ghost and the Printer's Baby."

Mrs. Stockton packed four large volumes with details of this long trip, and the record provided the material for an extensive series of travel papers, "Personally Conducted," which Stockton wrote for *St. Nicholas*. This travelogue for children reflects the skill with which Stockton earlier had illuminated the commonplace and the unusual in such collections as *Tales Out of School*. Stockton is as meticulous as Baedeker in giving facts concerning the countries he has visited, but he selects unerringly those essential national and racial differences which appeal to children, and those famous places of which every child has heard. The description in *Personally Conducted*, still valid and lively in 1889 when Scribners published it, was a shrewd selection of concrete details—dress, food, trains, carriages, habits—all well within the experience of children.

Upon their return from abroad, the Stocktons went directly to Philadelphia, to stay with Frank's brother, Colonel William S. Stockton. His sister Louise was ill, and he and Mrs. Stockton remained in Philadelphia until recovery permitted her to go to the Jersey shore for convalescence. Then the Stocktons went to Virginia, in the mountain country which Stockton had loved since he first saw it before his marriage when he visited Mary Ann Tuttle's relatives.

He was in better health than he had been for years. His sight was better as the result of treatments, and new glasses. For the first time in three years he was able to write his own letters with the old-fashioned quill pens which he preferred to cut himself. For short periods, too, he was able to read.

The last half of 1884 was memorable for the publication of three volumes by Scribners, *The Transferred Ghost* and *The Lady or the Tiger?*, both collections of short stories, and *The Story of Viteau*. Stockton began publication of "Personally Conducted" in *St. Nicholas* for November, and he had published, in September, one of his best known fanciful tales, "The Queen's Museum." In addition, he had won a prize of $500 for "An Unhistoric Page," as the best humorous story submitted in a contest conducted by *The Youth's Companion*.

The Lady or the Tiger? contained a group of short stories which Stockton had written within the previous two or three years and, besides "The Discourager of Hesitancy," contained "The Transferred Ghost" and its slight but quite amusing sequel, "The Spectral Mortgage," which brings back the former ghost of John Hinckman, now gaily garbed in the uniform of a Russian nobleman, to tell the distressed hero that the spectral mortgage on the haunted house will be taken over by another ghost. Some delicate satire on the disruption of a household attendant upon the arrival of a son is deftly included. The son, Pegram, a name the father loathes, but which was an honored one in Madeline's family, threatens to

"Pegramize" the household, and to send the father, who had romantically envisioned a lifelong companionship with his wife, "to talk to the old men." Young fathers, amazed and muted at being suddenly elbowed from the center of their wives' attention by the arrival of an insignificant bundle with an overdeveloped tendency toward midnight caterwauling, will be comforted by Stockton's sly satire.

"Our Story" (1883), included in the same volume, is a tale which at first reading leaves the reader staring at the last lines in blank wonderment. But a re-reading of the incidents reveals that Stockton has done—not wholly successfully—a daring thing. Two writers, the narrator of the tale and a young woman, decide to collaborate. They find suitable seclusion, and fall in love. But the story progresses admirably. A third writer, who lives in the same *pension,* seems omnipresent, and on several occasions saves the lovers from embarrassment. Their engagement is announced, and the necessity for the third writer's chaperonage disappears. The story concludes; "Our story was never finished. His was. This is it." The abrupt change from the subjective narration to the objective brings a shock to the reader's mind, and sends him back to consider the story in a new light.

If the year 1884 was a successful one for Stockton, it was but one of several years in which he was regularly writing memorable stories. But it was a year which saw the publication in book form, of an earlier *St. Nicholas* story which was not one of his better, more successful narratives. *The Story of Viteau,*[13] intended by Stockton to be a somewhat pretentious story of medieval life, fails to be impressive for the same reason that his later *The Buccaneers and Pirates of Our Coasts* was unsuccessful. Stockton could not write at his best when his imagination was tied down by geographical or historical circumstance. It cramped him and seemed to dampen those flights of fancy upon which so much of the charm of his stories depend. *The Story of Viteau* is workmanlike; Stock-

13 *St. Nicholas,* November 1882–April 1883.

ton's narrative skill saves it from dullness, but it is not up to the level of the *St. Nicholas* stories he was writing at this time.

The fullest expression of his imaginative fancy linked with shrewd common sense was paced by "The Queen's Museum," which appeared in *St. Nicholas Magazine* for September 1884. "The Queen's Museum" was one of the earliest of a group of stories, of which it later became the title piece, in which Stockton's youthful desire to domesticate the incredible was realized. It is a satire on the folly of attempting to regiment the interests of a people. The queen's "museum" contains a rare collection of buttonholes, and the queen is so passionately interested in buttonholes that she has decreed that all her subjects who are not interested in the museum will be cast into prison. An itinerant king arrives to discover the entire city imprisoned. Acting on the premise that different people like different things, and with the aid of an obliging band of robbers and an equally obliging magician, he stocks the museum with a collection in which there is something of interest to everyone. For good measure, he marries the queen. In the queen's apologia, Stockton has written as fine an exposition of the magpie instinct of the collector as appears anywhere:

For many years I have been a collector of button-holes; and there was nothing valuable or rare in the line of my studies of which I had not an original specimen or fac-simile. My agents brought me from foreign lands, even from the most distant islands of the sea, button-holes of every kind; in silk, in wool, in cloth of gold, in every imaginable material, and of those which could not be obtained careful copies were made. There was not a duplicate specimen in the whole collection; only one of each kind; nothing repeated.

Stockton was, as has elsewhere been indicated, a shrewd bargainer; his editorial experience had taught him the value of his work in the commercial market. He fully realized that his stories were in demand, and that he could command his own price. A letter to Mrs. Dodge, written about this time, marks a significant change in his attitude toward *St. Nicholas Magazine,* to which, in pecuniary matters, he had been generous because of the aid the magazine had given him in establishing himself as a free-lance writer.

Box 90
Charlottesville, Va.
July 30th/85

Dear Mrs. Dodge:

With this, I send you the Christmas story [14] I promised to write for St. N., and which I know ought to be in the editorial hands as soon as possible, if it is to be illustrated. It is not a fairy tale, but a "fanciful story." [15]

And now I wish to say a few words on the subject of prices. For some time past, I have been receiving from "outside" quarters, larger prices for my stories than from the Century Co. (I do not refer to "syndicates" where the prices are exceptional, and would not apply to magazines). Of course, I do not wish you to suppose that I have not been *entirely satisfied* with the rate ($100) heretofore agreed upon, but as my stories now command a higher price than that, I believe you will be just as willing to pay such increased price as anybody else. I have always been of the opinion that the price of the "short story" should bear a better proportion to that of an installment of a serial (merit being equal) than it now does.

What do you think of $150 for a story for a single number?

I now leave the matter in your hands and shall be very glad to have your opinion upon it.

Yours very truly
Frank R. Stockton

It is to be assumed that Stockton's "suggestion" was accepted, for he continued to appear regularly in *St. Nicholas.*

"Old Pipes and the Dryad," [16] his next story of interest, is written in the manner of his earlier fairy tales, but told with

14 "Christmas Before Last," *St. Nicholas,* Vol. XIII (December 1885), pp. 124–134.

15 Stockton's distinction seems to be that a "fairy tale" is simply a narrative of probable improbabilities, while a "fanciful story" is a narrative, intended for mature appreciation, in which, under his highly imaginative humor, are secreted his own acute observations of life.

16 *St. Nicholas,* Vol. XII (June 1885), pp. 561–568.

a mature poetic quality which raises it above the ordinary. The simple story of kindly, honest people, and an aging piper who is kissed by a dryad, it exhibits once again Stockton's supreme ability to make the trivial important. Each kiss of a dryad takes ten years from a man's age, and the piper and his mother are restored to vigor and health by a grateful dryad, whom the piper had released from imprisonment in her tree. Stockton's concept of the churlish Echo-dwarf is one of his happiest pictures.

But charming as is "Old Pipes and the Dryad," its interest is dwarfed in comparison with his next fanciful tale, "The Griffin and the Minor Canon," a story containing Stockton's nearest approach to bitterness and misanthropy through his sweeping indictment of men's selfishness and cowardice. It tells one of his little truths, so engagingly presented that the moral is not fully understood until the stinging last lines. In a wooded fastness, far from a quiet cathedral town, there dwelt a Griffin. Learning that his image was carved on the cathedral, and amiably curious concerning his own appearance, the Griffin flew to the city to inspect the gargoyle. His arrival threw the citizenry into a state of terror, and although the Griffin was pacific, of all the people only the Minor Canon of the Cathedral had the courage to meet it.

The Minor Canon, who filled a subordinate position in the old church, had just finished the afternoon services, and was coming out of a side door, with three aged women who had formed the week-day congregation, and very anxious to do good to the people of the town. Apart from his duties in the church, where he conducted services every week-day, he visited the sick and the poor, counselled and assisted persons who were in trouble, and taught a school composed entirely of the bad children in the town with whom nobody else would have anything to do. Whenever the people wanted something difficult done for them, they always went to the Minor Canon.

Charitable, kind, possessing that real courage which conquers fear while hands and knees still tremble, the Minor Canon goes to speak to the monster, "for it would be a woeful

thing if injury should come to the people of the town because he was not brave enough to obey the summons of the
Griffin." Epitomizing those rare and valiant souls who con-
scientiously do the dangerous, or the unpopular thing, and
by their greatness of soul give stature and dignity to human
life, the Minor Canon is one of Stockton's best-drawn and
most significant portraits. The Griffin gazes raptly at his stone
image, and soon becomes attached to the Minor Canon, following him like a tame puppy on the rounds of his duties. In
abject terror, the people force the Minor Canon to seek the
wilds from which the Griffin came, in the hope that the monster would follow him. The Minor Canon departs without
telling the Griffin, and disconsolately the great beast tries to
fulfill his duties, teaching the Minor Canon's school, visiting
the sick and the poor. The results are all that might be expected. The pupils become model scholars, the sick recover
miraculously, and the poor, hitherto utterly dependent upon
charity, find jobs.

But the autumnal equinox was approaching, and the people became alarmed, since the equinox was the only time at
which the Griffin fed. They offer to prepare a banquet for
him, but he refuses because the Minor Canon, "who is brave
and good and honest," is the only creature in the town the
Griffin could relish. He learns of their trick in sending the
Minor Canon away, and, so furious his tail becomes red-hot,
he angrily summons the citizens to a meeting.

When everybody who was able to come was there, the Griffin
stood still and addressed the meeting.

"I have had a contemptible opinion of you," he said, "ever
since I discovered what cowards you are, but I had no idea that
you were so ungrateful, selfish, and cruel, as I now find you to be.
Here was your Minor Canon, who labored day and night for
your good, and thought of nothing else but how he might benefit you and make you happy; and as soon as you imagine yourselves threatened with a danger,—for well I know you are dread-
fully afraid of me,—you send him off, caring not whether he
returns or perishes, hoping thereby to save yourselves."

He threatens terrible destruction if, when the Canon returns, the people do not put him in the highest place and serve and honor him all his life. Departing, and taking the stone griffin with him, the Griffin returns to his wilds, where he finds the Minor Canon, weak and half starved. The story blends now into a more mellow, more typically Stocktonian tone as the Griffin and the Minor Canon converse. The effective device by which Stockton soberly recounts the incredible is here at its most appealing.

"Do you know," said the monster, when he had finished, "that I have had, and still have a great liking for you?"

"I am very glad to hear it," said the Minor Canon, with his usual politeness.

"I am not at all sure that you would be," said the Griffin, "if you thoroughly understood the state of the case, but we will not consider that now. If some things were different, some things would be otherwise."

Regretfully, for the autumnal equinox is rapidly approaching, the Griffin returns the Minor Canon to the town, where the people, remembering the Griffin's fearful threats, heap honors upon the gentle curate.

But they need never have been afraid of the Griffin. The autumnal equinox day came round, and the monster ate nothing. If he could not have the Minor Canon, he did not care for anything. So, lying down, with his eyes on the great stone griffin, he gradually declined, and died. It was a good thing for some of the people of the town that they did not know this.

Thus, with a last word for backsliders, Stockton concludes one of his greatest stories, one of the very few stories in which he is really concerned with the depiction of the seamy side of human nature. The story is full of happy phrases, and Stockton's "fancy" seldom has had such material to work on. "The Griffin and the Minor Canon" makes it clear that Stockton was no mere idle teller of idle stories; that "he saw life clearly, and saw it whole." "The Griffin and the Minor Canon" is as thoroughgoing an indictment of herd-fear and herd-malice as we have in American literature.

A gentle satire on the stupidity of changing people who are satisfied as they are into something else is the title story of a volume issued in 1887, "The Bee-Man of Orn," [17] which originally appeared in *St. Nicholas* as "The Bee-Man and His Original Form."

The Bee-Man, poor, ugly, untidy, learns from a Junior Sorcerer that he has been transformed, and that he ought to be changed back. The Junior Sorcerer, asked by the Bee-Man from what he had been transformed, gives an answer characteristic of all such tinkerers with other people's lives:

"That is more than I know," said the Junior Sorcerer. "But one thing is certain—you ought to be changed back. If you will find out what you have been transformed from, I will see that you are made all right again. Nothing will please me better than to attend to such a case."

The Bee-Man's contentment disappears, and he sets out on a journey to discover what he should be. He determines that, since he is drawn toward a baby which he rescues from a dragon, he must have been transformed from a baby. The Junior Sorcerer reappears and by his magic, changes the Bee-Man into a baby. Years afterward, the Sorcerer finds, deep in the woods of Orn, a bee-man whom he recognizes as the original Bee-Man. "Upon my word," said the Sorcerer, "he has grown into the same thing again!" The story is Stockton's expression of the notion that men, given the opportunity for change, will tend to revert to the familiar and the known, and that nature is timeless—and changeless.

Stockton was a regular contributor of Christmas stories to the periodicals for which he wrote. Beginning with "Stephen Skarridge's Christmas," an effective parody, told with a characteristic sobriety, on the perennial reappearance of Dickens' "Christmas Carol" under one guise or another, Stockton wrote a number of Christmas stories, which, as a group, are of a quality superior to the usual type of this patterned "good will to men" plot.

[17] *St. Nicholas*, Vol. XI (November 1883), pp. 46–52.

"The Christmas Before Last," [18] the saga of the erratic voyage of the *Horn o' Plenty,* is a truly Stocktonian approach to Christmas cheer. There is, however, a deeper significance in Stockton's treatment of the idea of "the fruit of the fragile palm," fruit so rare that it is universally sought, and prized for its rarity. The boys of the First Class in Long Division, who have been rescued by Captain Covajos of the *Horn o' Plenty,* solve the problem of obtaining the fruit in true boy fashion.

"Prince Hassak's March" [19] tells of the erratic journey of Prince Hassak from the city of Itoby to the city of Yan, after he has decided that a mighty prince ought not go out of his way for mountains or rivers, or respect the rights of those who conflict with his whims. The plight of the jailor who has had no prisoners for fourteen years, the red-bearded man anxious to form a nucleus, and the Pigwidgeons, anxious to divide five-sevenths by six, are good touches.

"The Battle of the Third Cousins" [20] opens on a note of satire:

There were never many persons who could correctly bound the Autocracy of Mutjado. The reason for this was that the boundary line was not stationary. Whenever the Autocrat felt the need of money, he sent his tax-gatherers far and wide, and people who up to that time had no idea of such a thing found that they lived in the territory of Mutjado. But when times were ordinarily prosperous with him, and people in the outlying districts needed protection or public works, the dominion of the Autocrat became very much contracted.

From national economy, Stockton's barb shifts to doctors who practise by the trial-and-error method, and to faddists, in the person of old Salim, who, to prolong life, shifts his masticatory count from thirty-two per mouthful to thirty-six.

"The Banished King" [21] satirizes the idea of autocratic gov-

18 *St. Nicholas,* Vol. XIII (December 1885), pp. 124–134.
19 *St. Nicholas,* Vol. XI (December 1883), pp. 141–150.
20 *St. Nicholas,* Vol. XII (September 1885), pp. 809–815.
21 *St. Nicholas,* Vol. X (December 1882), p. 118–126.

ernment, with a barbed account of people who can never
make up their minds.

"Now," said the King to the Sphinx, "I am in favor of moving
on. I am tired of this place, where every sentiment is so mingled
with others that you can never tell what anybody really thinks
or feels. I don't believe anyone in this country was ever truly
glad or sorry. They mix one sentiment so quickly with another
that they never can discover the actual ingredients of any of
their impulses."

"When this King first began to mingle his sentiments," said
the Sphinx, "it was because he always desired to think and feel
exactly right. He did not wish his feelings to run too much one
way or the other."

"And so he is never either right or wrong," said the King.

This group of short "fanciful tales," as Stockton called
them, were written at a time when Stockton was reaching
the zenith of his powers. His audience was shifting from the
readers of *St. Nicholas* to the more general magazines, and he
wrote but few such stories after "The Christmas Before Last"
(December 1885). None of them approached the charm and
the deftness of understatement, the shrewd readings of life,
and the very real beauty of such stories as "The Griffin and
the Minor Canon," "The Bee-Man of Orn," and "Old Pipes
and the Dryad." They represent a phase of Stockton's work
which made contributions to the literature of the world.
They are timeless, they are, in their simplicity, and in their
amazing complexity, in their humanity, and in their gentle
humor, a rich addition to our American literature, and to the
gentle wisdom of the world. As has been indicated, these early
years of the 80's were among Stockton's most productive. He
had not yet written a novel, and was anxious to write a story
in the longer form. During 1885, most of which he spent in
Virginia, at Painesville, he began his first novel. Through
the spring and summer, he lay at ease in a hammock slung
between two trees, dictating the story, *The Late Mrs. Null*.

Stockton's methods of working were peculiar. For two or
three hours in the morning he dictated his story to an aman-

uensis. During the rest of the day he loafed, puttered around the garden, went driving, chatted with neighbors and friends, the while he constantly thought out the matter for tomorrow's dictation. He conceived plot sequence, details of characterization, even dialogue, before he spoke a word. The result was a slow-paced flow of narrative, with but occasional pauses while he untangled some knotty problem of plot or dialogue. He seldom, apparently, made revisions once the story had been dictated, a fact which may account for such a loosely constructed and tediously detailed story as *The Hundredth Man*. It accounts for such errors as the fact that *The Late Mrs. Null* gives, on one page "an honest straightforward look from her *grey* eyes," and, later, she "fixed on him her large *blue* eyes," and perhaps for such an error as occurs in *Kate Bonnet*, "It was a bright morning when, with a fair wind on her bright *starboard bow,* the sloop Belinda sailed southward." Had he revised with reasonable care, Stockton was enough of a sailor to have remarked the spectacle of a ship sailing backward!

Slow-moving, because of Stockton's interest in incident, often at the expense of plot and movement, *The Late Mrs. Null* [22] is nevertheless a novel of considerable charm. Lawrence Croft, supposing himself in love with Roberta Marsh, the niece of Robert Brandon, decides to investigate the character of Junius Keswick, whose engagement to Roberta had been broken through the efforts of Junius' aunt, Mrs. Keswick. Croft interests Annie Peyton, the niece of Mrs. Keswick, who as "Mrs. Null" undertakes the investigation. The disguise of "Mrs. Null" is necessitated by the desire of Annie Peyton to avoid her domineering aunt, and to obtain the liberty of movement which the supposed existence of a husband will give her. As the story progresses, Lawrence Croft falls in love with Annie, while Annie, as "Mrs. Null," aids the romance of Roberta Marsh and Junius Keswick. At the novel's end the two pairs of lovers are happily united, while

22 *The Late Mrs. Null,* New York, 1886, 1891, 1907.

only misery awaits old Mr. Brandon, who has long been the object of Mrs. Keswick's terrible, unforgiving hatred.

Mrs. Keswick, another of those elderly women whom Stockton drew so skillfully, is the dominant figure in the novel. She is a woman who knows her own mind, and who is ruthless in the means she uses to achieve her desires. Stockton tells us what she is through the description which Uncle Isham, a Negro, gives in answer to Junius Keswick's question:

"I suppose," said the young man, "that as she went away on foot she must be staying with some of the neighbors. If we were to make inquiries, it certainly would not be difficult to find out where she is."

"Mahs' Junius," said Uncle Isham, his black eyes shining brighter and brighter as he spoke, "dar's cullud people, an' white folks too, in dis yere county who'd put on der bes' clothes an' black der shoes, an' skip off wid alacrousness, to do de wus kin' o' sin, dat dey knowed for sortin would send 'em down to de deepes' an' hottes' gullies ob de lower regions, but nuffin in dis worl' could make one o' dem people go 'quirin' 'bout ole miss when she didn't want to be 'quired about."

Mrs. Keswick is indeed a terrible woman. She has driven her husband to suicide, and broken off the engagement of her nephew, Junius Keswick. She had so antagonized her brother, Annie Peyton's father, that when he died Annie was too proud, and too loyal to her father, to seek help from Mrs. Keswick. She prefers to work for her living, and it is through her position in Candy's Information Shop that Lawrence Croft meets her. Mrs. Keswick has long hated Mr. Brandon, Roberta's uncle, a hatred of which he has been unaware, and the scene in which she opens her campaign of revenge is one of the highlights of the story.

Mr. Brandon was seated in an arm chair by a table, and not very far from a wood fire of a size suited to the season. His slippered feet were on a cushioned stool; his eye-glasses were carefully adjusted on the capacious bridge of his nose; and, intent upon a newspaper which had arrived by that morning's mail, he presented the appearance of a very well satisfied old gentleman, in very comfortable circumstances. But when he turned his head and saw the Widow Keswick close the door behind her, every idea of satisfaction or comfort seemed to vanish from his mind. He dropped the paper; he rose to his feet; he took off his eyeglasses; he turned somewhat red in the face; and he ejaculated: "What! madam! So it is you, Mrs. Keswick?"

The old lady did not immediately answer. Her head dropped a little on one side, a broad smile bewrinkled the lower part of her well-worn visage, and with her eyes half-closed, behind her heavy spectacles, she held out both her hands, the purple umbrella in one of them, and exclaimed in a voice of happy fervor: "Robert! I am yours!"

Mr. Brandon, recovered from his surprise, had made a step forward to go round the table and greet his visitor; but at these words he stopped as if he had been shot. Perception, understanding, and even animation, seemed to have left him as he vacantly stared at the elderly female with purple sun-bonnet and umbrella, blue calico gown, red shawl and coarse boots, who held out her arms towards him, and who gazed upon him with an air of tender, though decrepit, fondness.

"Don't you understand me, Robert?" she continued. "Don't you remember the day, many a good long year ago, it is true, when we walked together down there by the branch, and you asked me to be yours? I refused you, Robert, and, although you went down on your knees in the damp grass and besought me to give me your heart, I would not do it. But I did not know you then as I know you now, Robert, and the words of love which you spoke to me that morning come to me now with a sweetness which I was too young and trifling to notice then. That heart is yours now, Robert. I am yours." And, with these words, she made a step forward.

At this demonstration Mr. Brandon appeared suddenly to recover his consciousness and he precipitately made two steps backwards, just missing tumbling over his foot-stool into the fireplace.

"Madam!" he exclaimed, "what are you talking about?"

"Of the days of our courtship, and your love, Robert," she said. "My love did not come then, but it is here now. Here now," she repeated, putting the hand with the umbrella in it on her breast.

"Madam," exclaimed the old gentleman, "you must be raving

crazy! Those things to which you allude, happened nearly half a century ago; and since that you have been married and settled, and—"

"Robert," interrupted the Widow Keswick, "you are mistaken. It is not quite forty-five years since that morning, and why should hearts like ours allow the passage of time or the mere circumstance of what might be called an outside marriage, but now extinct, to come between them? There is many a spring, Robert, which does not show when a man first begins to dig, but it will bubble up in time. And, Robert, it bubbles now." And with her head bent a little downwards, although her eyes were still fixed upon him, she made another step in his direction.

Mr. Brandon now backed himself flat against some bookshelves in his rear. The perspiration began to roll from his face, and his whole form trembled. "Mrs. Keswick! Madam!" he exclaimed, "You will drive me mad!"

Mrs. Keswick forces marriage upon poor Mr. Brandon, and at the ceremony publicly humiliates him by answering, when the usual question was asked, "Not I! Marry that man there?" She castigates him mercilessly, and stalks with an air of satisfied vengeance from the church.

The scene of the novel is Paineville, Virginia, and Elmwood, three miles away. It was a setting with which Stockton was thoroughly familiar, for he had walked and driven through the country many times during his frequent stays with the Tuttles. Stockton's sympathy with the South is revealed in his understanding of the relations between Whites and Negroes, a mutual dependence built upon respect and an intuitive understanding of rights and privileges. The Negroes in *The Late Mrs. Null* are genuine people. Uncle Isham, Aunt Patsy, Aunt Patsy's son Tom's yellow boy Bob's child, and Peggy, are realistically described, and anyone who has had experience with the Southern Negro recognizes at once how justly Stockton has depicted them. The scene in which old Aunt Patsy, who has not set foot outside her cabin for fifteen years, gathers herself together by gargantuan labors to go and tell Mrs. Keswick, her "Ole Miss," what she thinks of her, is thoroughly in keeping with the domineering devotion and the undaunted loyalty of a fast disappearing type of servant, but one still common in Stockton's Virginia.

The Late Mrs. Null was a remarkably well-sustained narrative for one who had worked hitherto only in the somewhat specialized form of the short story. Picturesque episodes occur in the novel, but it is not episodic. Its whimsical humor produces situations which develop with more naturalness and spontaniety than is usual with Stockton. Annie Peyton, the "late Mrs. Null," is a charming, vital girl, and the men—Mr. Brandon, Junius Keswick, and Lawrence Croft—are more virile and personable than Stockton's male characters usually are. Mrs. Keswick may be a caricature, but in the story she looms distressingly like the sort of aunt of which each family possesses at least one. She is a very real and very terrible old woman.

Charming as are many of the episodes in *The Late Mrs. Null,* the public which had appreciated that novel did not expect Stockton to return to the manner of *Rudder Grange* for his next story. He did, however, take up again his method of sober narration of the extraordinary in terms of the commonplace. The story, *The Casting Away of Mrs. Lecks and Mrs. Aleshine* (1886) almost immediately became a minor classic. Like *Rudder Grange, The Casting Away of Mrs. Lecks and Mrs. Aleshine* was not originally intended in its present form. As a long short story, or novelette, it ran through three issues of the *Century Magazine,*[23] and ended on such a tantalizing note that a sequel was written to answer every reader's question, "What did the Dusantes do when they returned to find 'the wedding cards on the parlor table, not a speck of dust in any corner, and the board money in the ginger-jar'?" "The Dusantes" was published in the *Century* during December 1887, and January and February 1888.[24] In subsequent book publication the two stories were deftly joined, and the break between the parts is unnoticeable.

---

[23] *Century Magazine,* New Series, Vol. X (August, September, October, 1886), pp. 595, 706, 870.
[24] New Series, Vol. XIII, pp. 244, 385, 617.

The Casting Away of Mrs. Lecks and Mrs. Aleshine is one of Stockton's great stories. It is full of memorable moments, and Stockton never showed greater skill in sustaining the note of high comedy from incident to incident. Mrs. Lecks and Mrs. Aleshine are real persons, and represent the high-water mark of Stockton's characterizations. No bald synopsis can convey the delightful quality of humor with which Stockton has invested the story. Two middle-aged women, Mrs. Lecks and Mrs. Aleshine, from a small Pennsylvania village, set out from San Francisco to visit the latter's son in Japan. They encounter Mr. Craig, the narrator of the story, on shipboard. Somewhere in the Pacific the ship founders, and finding a lifeboat mysteriously but conveniently empty, they decide they will be more comfortable in it than in the other already crowded lifeboats. Left behind by the others, the three discover the reason their boat was empty—water is coming in faster than they can bail it out. The boat sinks, and using oars like brooms, Mrs. Lecks and Mrs. Aleshine make rapid progress in the wake of Mr. Craig toward an island which he has discovered. The island is uninhabited, but there is a handsome home, a full larder, a boat, and a garden, all of which the party commandeers. Solemnly, Mrs. Lecks and Mrs. Aleshine decide that the proper thing to do is to pay board to the absent owners. The scene may have been intended as a burlesque on the hackneyed stories of castaways *de luxe,* who find so many convenient items washed upon the shore, or in abandoned huts. Whatever its purpose, it has a humor all its own, and serves admirably to illuminate the contrasting yet complementary characters of the women.

"Now," continued Mrs. Lecks, "it's my opinion that we ought to pay our board regular every week. I don't know what is commonly charged in a place like this, but I know you can get very good board where I come from for six dollars a week."

"That is for two in a room," said Mrs. Aleshine; "but havin' a room to himself would make it more for Mr. Craig."

"It ain't his fault," said Mrs. Lecks, somewhat severely, "that he ain't got a brother or some friend to take part of the room and pay part of the expense. But anyway the room isn't a large one, and I don't think he ought to pay much more for havin' a room to himself. Seven dollars is quite enough."

"But then you've got to consider," said Mrs. Aleshine, "that we do the cookin' and housework, and that ought to be counted."

"I was comin' to that," said Mrs. Lecks. "Now, if me and Mrs. Aleshine was to go out to service, which you may be sure we wouldn't do unless circumstances was very different from what they are now—"

"That's true!" earnestly ejaculated Mrs. Aleshine.

"But if we was to do it," continued Mrs. Lecks, "we wouldn't go into anybody's family for less than two dollars a week. Now, I've always heard that wages is low in this part of the world, and the work isn't heavy for two of us; so, considering the family isn't here to make their own bargain, I think we'd better put our wages at that, so that'll make four dollars a week for each of us two to pay."

"But how about Mr. Craig?" said Mrs. Aleshine. "He oughtn't to work in that garden for nothin'.'"

"Fifty cents a day," said Mrs. Lecks, "is as little as any man would work for, and then it oughtn't to take all his time. That will make three dollars to take out of Mr. Craig's board, and leave it four dollars a week the same as ours."

I declared myself perfectly satisfied with these arrangements, but Mrs. Aleshine did not seem to be altogether convinced that they were just.

"When a woman goes out to service," said she, "she gets her board and is paid wages besides, and it's the same for gardeners."

"Then I suppose, Barb'ry Aleshine," said Mrs. Lecks, "that we ought to charge these people with our wages, and make 'em pay it when they come back!"

This remark apparently disposed of Mrs. Aleshine's objections, and her friend continued:

"There's a jar on the mantelpiece there, of the kind the East Indy ginger comes in. It's got nothin' in it now but some brown paper in which fish-hooks is wrapped. We came here on a Wednesday, and so every Tuesday night we'll each put four dollars in that jar, under the fish-hook paper; then, if, by night or by day, the family comes back and makes a fuss about our bein' here, all we have to say is, 'The board money's in the ginger-jar,' and our consciences is free."

The three castaways live comfortably in their island home until the arrival of the Reverend Mr. Enderton, his daughter, Ruth, and the three sailormen, the coxswain, Jim, and Bill. Ruth is a pretty, sheltered girl, whom Mrs. Lecks and Mrs. Aleshine immediately determine Mr. Craig should marry. Their methods are somewhat harsh, but their benevolent purpose is achieved rapidly. The three sailormen become attached to plump Mrs. Aleshine, and one of the happier episodes in the novel concerns their attempt to please her.

The party finally depart in the seaworthy boat in which Enderton and the sailors arrived, but not before Mrs. Lecks and Mrs. Aleshine have cleaned the Dusante home with housewifely thoroughness. The board money, including that collected from the parsimonious Rev. Mr. Enderton, is carefully left in the ginger-jar, with a note explaining the circumstances.

The second part of the story tells of some hilarious adventures of Mrs. Lecks, Mrs. Aleshine, the Craigs, and Mr. Enderton in the West, and of the meeting with the Dusantes— Mr. Dusante, his daughter, and his daughter's adopted mother —who, having returned to the island, discover the ginger-jar and set out to return it to their inadvertent guests. After a series of misadventures precipitated by the minister, the entire group ends up in Meadowville, Pennsylvania, the home of Mrs. Lecks and Mrs. Aleshine. There they are greeted by the three sailormen, the coxswain, Jim, and Bill, who adopt Mrs. Aleshine as their captain, to her intense pleasure.

One of Stockton's happiest scenes is that one with which the novel ends, the decoration of Mrs. Aleshine's farm:

One of the men had a pocket chart of the colors adopted by the different steamship companies all over the world, and now smoke houses, corn-cribs, chicken-houses, and so on, down to pumps and hitching-posts were painted in great bands of blue and red and white and black, arranged in alternating orders,

until an observer might have supposed that a commercial navy
had been sunk beneath Mrs. Aleshine's house grounds, leaving
nothing but its smoke-stacks visible.

The greatest work of decoration, however, was reserved by the
red-bearded coxswain for himself, designed by his own brain and
executed by his own hands. This was the tattooing of the barn.
Around this building, the sides of which were already of a color
sufficiently resembling a well-tanned human skin, the coxswain
painted in blue spots resembling tattooing an immense cable
passing several times about the structure, a sea-serpent almost as
long as the cable, eight anchors, two ships under full sail, with
a variety of cannons and flags which filled up the remaining
spaces. This great work was a long time in execution, and before
it was half-finished its fame had spread over the surrounding
country.

The Reverend Mr. Enderton, a caricature, but like many
of Dickens' caricatures, a very live one, is undoubtedly a
picture of Stockton's father, William Smith Stockton. The
description of Enderton epitomizes William Stockton's character:

He was a prim and somewhat formal man and appeared to be
entirely self-engrossed, with very vague notions in regard to his
surroundings. He was not by any means an ill-tempered man, being rather inclined to be passive than otherwise, but he gave so
little attention to circumstances and events that he did not appear
to understand why he should be incommoded by the happenings of life. . . . Mr. Enderton gave us very little of his company, for having discovered that there was a library in the house
he passed most of his time in that room.

"You have made a very fair selection of books, sir," he remarked to me, "but it may readily be conceived from the character of the works that your tastes are neither ecclesiastic nor
scientific."

Several times I explained to him the ownership of the library
and the house, but he immediately forgot what I had said or paid
no attention to it.[25]

25 Cf. *Poems: with Autobiographic and Other Notes* by T. H. Stockton,
Philadelphia, 1862, Chapter I, *passim*. And also (pp. 309–310): "Of course, the
religious spirit was always present with my father. . . . But he too, was re-

As with so much of Stockton's work, it is difficult for the commentator to convey the delicately humorous quality of *The Casting Away of Mrs. Lecks and Mrs. Aleshine*. Seemingly without effort, Stockton builds up his successive situations, and only a full knowledge of the characters can adequately convey the richness of the comedy evoked by his method of approaching the extraordinary, even the incredible, as if it were "what might have been expected." In a real sense, Mrs. Lecks and Mrs. Aleshine represent Stockton's method of developing whimsical humor. Middle-aged, practical housewives, who have never before left their village, they are prepared for the unusual and treat it as a commonplace. Who but Mrs. Lecks could have produced sausages and biscuits (dry, in a glass jar), and a bit of stimulating whisky, while swimming in the middle of the Pacific Ocean? Who but Mrs. Lecks would have thought of black stockings as a protection against sharks, because "sharks never bite colored people"? Who but Mrs. Aleshine would have thought of plying an oar as she would a broom, and so paddle herself through the ocean at a slow but steady rate? These two, Mrs. Lecks and Mrs. Aleshine, are real people. They are generous, kindly, honest, self-respecting. They meet unusual situations with what equipment they have, and their triumphs over circumstances are the result not of good fortune, but of intelligence and industry.[26] We remember them as delightful

markably fond of reading, and probably the more so because of his embarrassment in talking. He had an extraordinary reverence for authors. I have learned from him, that, one day, as he was coming to the house from the garden, where he had been sitting in the shade communing with some pleasant writer, he concluded that he would rather be the author of a good book than gain anything else the world could give. Some of the Friends . . . noticed his love of books and kindly invited him to the use of their library—a favor to which he often gratefully alluded, and which he so improved as to acquire the highest esteem for 'solid' Quakers." The characters of Mr. Stockton and "Mr. Enderton" are similar at too many points for them to be other than model and picture.

26 Arthur Hobson Quinn, in his *American Fiction* (New York, 1936) sees in their very names an index to their characters—*lex*, law, and *Allshine*, reflection (p. 227). Since Stockton himself enjoyed Latin tags, *lex* is probably the correct origin. But in an old MS notebook of Stockton's there is an entry, dated August 22, 1880, recording payment of $2.50 for board and lodging to

persons, and we laugh at the incongruity of the situations in which they get themselves. But our laughter is friendly; we share their interest in the unknown owner of the island home; we admire their courage, their industry, their honesty. We share their indignation at the churlish selfishness of Mr. Enderton, and we know the pleasure Mrs. Aleshine takes in the attachment of her three sailormen. We are as anxious as Mrs. Lecks to return the ginger-jar to its owner, Mr. Dusante. They are real women, plain folks, but independent and genuine. We laugh at them, but we respect them. They are truly placed among the great heroines of American fiction.

The publication of *The Casting Away of Mrs. Lecks and Mrs. Aleshine* capped a decade during which Stockton had become successively more in demand as a contributor to American magazines. He had made the most of one great talent, an ability to project unimaginative people into incongruous or extraordinary situations, and evoke therefrom a whimsical, quiet humor which has a universal appeal. In the remaining fourteen years of his life he became a major figure among contemporary novelists, but he never again wholly recaptured the charm of *Rudder Grange, The Floating Prince*, "The Lady, or the Tiger?" "The Griffin and the Minor Canon," and *The Casting Away of Mrs. Lecks and Mrs. Aleshine*. After his death his reputation dwindled measurably, and he is now remembered chiefly by a handful of stories which, written mostly during the eighties, are definite contributions to our literature.

But in the period of which we write, Stockton's literary star was in the ascendant, and he was preparing a new type of story, the imaginative picture of the future, the story of the pseudo-scientific. It was a change of pace, not of manner or material. The same imagination which could conceive the adventures of Mrs. Lecks and Mrs. Aleshine, which could write of ghosts and fairies as if they were common folk, was not an imagination easily to be outdistanced by Jules Verne.

"Mrs. Aleshine," in an unspecified place. Also, on January 15, 1881, Stockton notes $20.00 paid to a "Mrs. Shine" for board in Florida.

In 1888, therefore, Stockton faced a bright future, his material by no means exhausted, his reputation growing with every story published. If his finest work was behind him, he could not have known that, and he was yet to create some memorable people who would meet some astonishing things with the serenity of the male Rudder Granger, and the dignity and poise of Mrs. Lecks and Mrs. Aleshine.

Chapter VI

Upon their return from the southern trip the Stocktons lived at Morristown, New Jersey. The days were full ones for Stockton. He was writing busily, dictating from nine until one o'clock every day, and he was riding the crest of popularity achieved by his longer stories. The last installment of *The Casting Away of Mrs. Lecks and Mrs. Aleshine* was published in the October 1886 issue of the *Century*, and in November the first installment of *The Hundredth Man* appeared. The serial ran for a full year, the last section appearing in October 1887.

The Hundredth Man is definitely below the level of excellence of *The Late Mrs. Null*. It is a long, often tedious, story of the search of Horace Stratford for "the hundredth man," the rare and unusual individual whose qualities of honesty, intelligence and industry make him stand out from the ninety-and-nine.

It had come to him in the course of his reading and thought, that in every hundred books on a kindred subject, in every hundred crimes of a similar kind, in every hundred events of a like nature, and in every hundred men who may come within one's cognizance, there is one book, crime, circumstance or man which stands up above and distinct from the rest, pre-eminent in the fact that no one of the others is, or could have been, like it.

Upon the shoulders of this rhetorical exposition of the obvious, Stockton rears a massive story, slow moving and dull. The endless details concerning "Vatoldi's" are interesting only in so far as they represent expression of Stockton's interest in restaurants, and in the preparation of food. Stockton's whole life was so temperate that there is something of the incongruous in his interest in restaurants, but they were, nevertheless, a hobby. During his usual long stay in New York in the winter, he and Mrs. Stockton made frequent excursions in search of new restaurants with much the same enthusiasm another type of person brings to the collections of first editions. But, apart from this, *The Hundredth Man* has little to offer. We are not interested in the search for the unusual individual because the search is speculative, unmotivated, and unimportant.

In December 1887 and January 1888, Stockton published in *St. Nicholas* a pleasant story, "The Clocks of Rondaine," the title of which was suggested by the clocks of Avignon, which, Stockton said, "I used to hear at night, striking when they had a mind to."

A letter to Mary Mapes Dodge, with whom he was in constant correspondence because of the number of his stories which she published in *St. Nicholas,* reveals implicitly Stockton's feeling that his "fanciful tales" were not appreciated by the audience for which they were really intended.

One of the drawbacks [he says] in writing a fanciful story, is the probable difficulty of finding a suitable person to read it. This drawback, however, does not trouble me—when I send a story up to the lower end of Central Park [Mrs. Dodge's home], I am quite sure that it will not lack a suitable reader. Charles Scribner's Sons have just published a volume of stories which I have reason to believe would not have been written had not the author felt sure that there was the right sort of sympathy at the other end of the line.

Stockton referred to the stories in *The Queen's Museum,* which had just been published.

Stockton's next long story, less bulky and with more movement than *The Hundredth Man,* was *Amos Killbright: His Adscititious Experience,* a title which sent his readers scurrying to their dictionaries. Amos Killbright convinces a young attorney that he is the materialized spirit of a man who had died in 1785. He is the virtual slave of an unscrupulous spiritualistic experimenter who intends to exploit him. The lawyer gives him work, and Amos, settling down to his new life, falls in love. But a German psychologist has perfected a method of dematerialization, and uses it on Killbright's wedding day. His protector's wife, naturally sympathetic to romance, gives the psychologist a going-over in the fashion of outraged femininity, and he hastily materializes Amos in time for the wedding. The contrast which Amos finds between 1785 and 1885 (when the story was probably written) provides some interesting moments.

Amos Killbright was probably a study for *The Vizier of the Two Horned Alexander* (1899) in which a number of amusing incongruities appear. The basic idea of the Wandering Jew is a particularly stimulating one, since it affords the romantic novelist so many opportunities, with few restrictions. Mr. Crowder, a man of fifty-three, protests that in Abraham's time he was the Vizier of the Two-Horned Alexander, and that having by mistake drunk the waters of Shem, which confer immortality, he has lived through the centuries since. He has met Moses, who "asked embarrassing questions"; he was a fellow clerk with Charles Lamb at India House; he has been a Carthusian monk; he has had fourteen of his books burned in the destruction of the library at Alexandria; he has been a broker in Pompeii; and he has helped Herodotus with his history. Thus, in cheerful disregard for the laws of mortality and the tyranny of time, has Crowder rambled through the ages. Many of the episodes which Crowder narrates so soberly are genuinely humorous, but it is difficult to determine whether Stockton intends to burlesque the theme of the Wandering Jew, or whether he is simply making use of the possibilities which such a theme affords him to escape once more from the everyday world, and permit his fancy free play. But precisely because his attitude is farcical, *The Vizier of the Two-Horned Alexander* makes stimulating, as well as amusing, reading. The great of the past, caught at inopportune moments, lose none of their greatness and gain in humanity, and Stockton's method of relating the story with a calm, circumstantial air gives it additional charm as an intellectual and historical holiday.

For the story "The Curious History of a Message," which appeared in *St. Nicholas* for December, Stockton adopted a unique method of determining the price. He suggested that, since the story would run ten columns, and each column would be more interesting than the one before it, he be paid only fifty cents for the first column, one dollar for the second, two dollars for the third, etc., a method which would bring the total price to $511.50! Cannily Mrs. Dodge replied (September 14, 1888):

After your quizzical proposition, which gave us our heartiest laugh of the season, we cannot, of course, put ourselves in the position of "beating down" so noble a contributor. No, rather let us raise upon him. He proposes to begin with fifty cents a column. We shall make it fifty dollars,—only, we shall start at the other end—paying fifty dollars for the final column, twenty-five for the ninth; twelve and a half for the eighth, and so on, halving as the interest decreases. Then, lest this plan may not quite meet the author's views, we are lavishly ready to throw in a couple of hundred dollars or so, for the title and name, which after all, are what most people read. Could anything be fairer than that?

Seriously, will you not name a definite price for "The Curious History of a Message," so that we may send the check at once?

Stockton asked $300, which was paid. The phrase which Mrs. Dodge uses, "throw in a couple of hundred dollars or so, for the title and name," is interesting, since it reflects her knowledge of Stockton's great popularity. He was now, in 1888, a well-known author, and notices concerning him were constantly appearing in literary journals. He was forced to submit to many interviews, which he did with grace and courtesy. In most, however, he had little to say, so that interviewers were often forced to concoct paragraphs similar to this:

The usual disorder of manuscripts, papers and books, [in Stockton's library] is conspicuously absent, and we look in vain for some justification of the averment of a visitor, that, while the touch of the lady is seen in the other apartments, the tiger evidently holds undisputed sway in the study.[1]

Actually, Stockton was not a very stimulating subject. There was a certain aloofness in his attitude which prevented any interviewer from asking questions other than the most obvious. The reason for this apparent aloofness was simply that of matters concerning literature, the trends and development of contemporary letters, the aims of his fellow members of the Authors Club, he was almost completely uninformed. The work of others was a matter of indifference to him; he seldom philosophized about his own work, and he had little ability at self-analysis or self-criticism. He wrote with a motive, but he seldom analyzed the means by which he achieved the effect he sought. Stockton did, however, on one or two occasions discuss his method. In answer to the question, "How do you go about laying out a story?" he replied:

First I lasso an idea. It may be a startling climax—an effect, the causes leading up to which will of themselves develop a narrative. With the main idea fast in my possession, the rest is comparatively easy. I plan the story generally in my head, though I sometimes sketch it out roughly on a sheet or two of paper. I never take the trouble to work out the details. I crowd the interest in characters toward a certain fixed point in the narrative.

Occasionally they protest and declare that they would not do what I make them do. Generally I like to see a character. I like a physical type, but I never copy anybody. Yet, strangely, I have to think of some face, of some acquaintance. The moral character is worked up by selecting traits from various men or women known to me.

By combining antithetical characteristics I produce some curious varieties, just as the nurseryman succeeds in changing the colors of his flowering plants. The number of varieties that can be conjured up are infinite. Take, for example, the characteristics of any two ladies among your acquaintance, antithetical as to their temperaments; amalgamate them into one personality, and then begin to invent a line of conduct for her. You will be surprised to find how differently from either of the two individual

[1] Edith M. Thomas in *McClure's,* Vol. I (November 1893), p. 467.

entities the new creature of your handiwork will act. I dislike
to rely on reading, because the ideas evolved are the offsprings of
another mind. I always feel however new the thought that comes
to me may be, that the author I am reading had had it in his
mind and rejected it.[2]

It may be an unfair criticism to accuse an author such as
Stockton, who was concerned primarily with narrative, of
having written stories and novels without any deep philosophical import. But many of his novels, like *The Hundredth
Man, Ardis Claverden,* and *The House of Martha,* propose
no very important conflict, such as would naturally result
from an author's strong convictions. One result is that, however "moral," however whimsical the characters Stockton
creates, the stories seem to lack force, and many remain comparatively unimportant—and unremembered. "The Lady, or
the Tiger?" endures because Stockton proposed an important
question in human behavior; Mrs. Lecks and Mrs. Aleshine
are important and memorable because they are so very *real*
that their actions become interesting. We are interested in
them as people, and the narrative of their casting away becomes an important problem. We want to know how they
meet and conquer the untoward circumstances into which
the sinking ship has thrust them. But in straightforward narrative and in the creation of incident, Stockton had developed
remarkable ability. For a new group of stories he added an
inventive imagination which produced what was for him a
wholly new type of story.

In writing a humorous story, "A Tale of Negative Gravity," [3] Stockton had "invented" a device, which, supported on
the wearer's back by shoulder straps, nullified the pull of
gravity, and permitted the wearer to rise or descend at will.
This device, circumspectly described, was the first of a series
of remarkable "inventions" which, in the light of later development, represent extraordinary foresight.

Using the method of Jules Verne, the combination of ad-

2 Quoted by Julius Chamber, in *Author,* Vol. III (July 15, 1891), p. 101.
3 *Century,* Vol. XXIX (November 1884), p. 135.

venture with popular science, and, apparently, the general
ideas which Verne had used in *A Journey to the Centre of the
Earth* (1864) and *Twenty Thousand Leagues under the Sea*
(1869), Stockton wrote two pseudo-scientific stories whose interest is still durable. Although they were written ten years
apart, *The Great War Syndicate* [4] and the *Great Stone of
Sardis* (1898) are very similar in type. Both reveal the fact
that Stockton's imaginative faculty was not limited to the
creation of the whimsical and the fanciful.

The Great War Syndicate is an imaginative narrative of a
naval war between the United States and Great Britain. To
the indignation of the War Department, the Navy Department, and the general public, the Government places the
conduct of the war in the hands of a War Syndicate, composed
of a group of capitalists in whose possession are hitherto unknown methods of waging scientific warfare. Great Britain is
speedily brought to terms by the terrible weapons used by
the syndicate. One of these, known as a Repeller, is a steel-
plated and bomb-proofed vessel which carries a single long-
range gun mechanically synchronized for aiming and firing
accurately, despite the pitch and roll of the ship, a projectile
of tremendous destructive force. [5] In addition to this terrible
weapon, the War Syndicate has a number of smaller ships,
known as "Crabs." Almost submerged, heavily armored, these
ships have strong steel pincers at their prows, with which they
are able to rip away the rudders and propellers of the might-
iest dreadnaughts which Great Britain boasts. The war ends
with the loss of only one life—and that loss is accidental. Great
Britain, after a repeated demonstration of the power and
indestructibility of the "Repellers" and "Crabs," joins the
United States in the Anglo-American War Syndicate, pledged
to make the world safe for its citizens.

The Great War Syndicate is a most interesting example of
the pseudo-scientific adventure story. Stockton has prophesied
such things as steel torpedo-nets, and huge howitzers capable

4 *Once a Week,* Vol. II, December 22, *et seq.,* 1888–1889.
5 Such a device to insure accurate naval firing has recently been invented.

of throwing a projectile for many miles. These things, now so commonplace as to arouse little interest, must have seemed to Stockton's readers as incredible as the British tanks seemed to the German General Staff before Cambrai. The interest in *The Great War Syndicate* naturally centers entirely in the description of Stockton's weapons to end war. That the action still is thrilling is as much a tribute to Stockton's narrative skill as it is to the inventions he describes.

Even more remarkable than *The Great War Syndicate* is *The Great Stone of Sardis,* the scene of which is laid in and about New York in the year 1947. A scientist and inventor, Roger Clews, operating from his workshop in Sardis, New Jersey, invents and equips a submarine which he sends to the North Pole. Connected by telegraphic cable with its New Jersey base (for even Stockton could not have conceived of radio communication in the state of electrical knowledge in 1897), Clews's submarine discovers and charts the North Pole without difficulty. While the submarine plows its way under ice fields, Clews and his scientifically minded fiancée, Margaret Raleigh, are experimenting with an artesian ray which, when focused, gradually penetrates the successive strata of the earth, until Clews, looking through the strongest telescope, can discern nothing but light. While he is puzzling over this condition fourteen miles within the earth, a huge projectile, invented for the construction of tunnels, breaks from its supporting frame and plunges into the ground. By the aid of his telescope, Clews discovers that the projectile has come to rest at that luminous point within the earth beyond which his artesian ray cannot penetrate. Descending into the great well by means of a cable car, Clews finds that the center of the earth is a tremendous diamond. He fills the shaft, lest the economic world be thrown off balance by unlimited quantities of diamonds thrown on the markets.

The many ways in which Stockton anticipated later discoveries will be readily apparent to any reader who has followed the development of practical science during the past two decades. Stockton's own knowledge of the scientific thought of his time was limited: all the material for *The Great War Syndicate* and *The Great Stone of Sardis* was taken from the *Encyclopedia Britannica*. What Stockton did was simply to exercise that logical faculty he possessed so definitely, and blend with his logical projection of ideas his imaginative and narrative faculties. The result was an anticipation of many things discovered or invented years later. Stockton's primary purpose was to write a good adventure tale; he was not interested as much in presenting an imaginative *tour de force* as he was in creating devices which would be dramatic and unusual, and hence excellent material for the teller of tales. It is not unreasonable to suppose that Thomas A. Edison, whose New Jersey laboratories were not far from Stockton's home, was the model for Roland Clews. Edison was, in 1897, perfecting a method, perhaps the most valuable of his contributions, of inventing methods of invention, and in the pages describing Roland Clews many projects imply just this development. It would be an interesting excursion to discover whether the notion was Stockton's alone—in which case it would be a discovery of tremendous importance—or whether he but reflected the scientific attitude of his time. In any event, apart from the intrinsic story-interest possessed by *The Great War Syndicate* and *The Great Stone of Sardis*, it is evident that Stockton possessed the realistic imagination of the inventor, and that many of his ideas, necessitated by the exigencies of the narrative, were prophetic foreshadowings of twentieth-century developments.

In 1890, Stockton purchased The Holt, at Convent Station, on the outskirts of Morristown, New Jersey, from Alfred E. Mills, a longtime friend. The Holt was, in a sense, the fulfillment of a long-standing ambition. It had extensive grounds, it was a large, rambling structure, on the roof of which was perched a cupola room in which Stockton enjoyed working. In the new house he and Mrs. Stockton, with whatever secretary was then current, lived their placid country life. He kept the guest rooms filled with his friends, with his nieces and nephews, with visiting celebrities. At fifty-six, Stockton was a person of prominence in contemporary letters, and he was reaping the fruits of his long career in just the way he most desired.

Mary Mapes Dodge discovered for him the name of his new home, and he had the two lines from George Turberville (1540?–1610?):

> *Yee that frequent the hilles and highest*
> *Holts of All*
> *Assist me with your skillful Quilles and listen when I call*

inscribed on the mantelpiece in the study in which he worked in winter or inclement weather. Across the field adjoining Stockton's property lived A. B. Frost, who illustrated so many of his stories, and was one of his few intimates. It was within easy access of New York, to which Mr. and Mrs. Stockton went for a part of each winter. On the grounds was a barn in which his horses could be stabled, and the surrounding familiar countryside was one he loved to drive through in winter as well as in summer. Although his tastes were always modest, he was fond of sleek driving horses, and the proceeds of several of his stories went into the purchase of blooded horses. On the grounds of The Holt there was also a small caretaker's cottage, occupied by Stockton's handyman and gardener, Joseph. Stockton was experiencing fully his long-cherished desire, expressed in his youth in "What Can I Do for an Old Gentleman,"

His wants being few and his tastes rural, he intended after he had made himself sufficiently known in the literary world, to retire to some country place, (not his native village) and there enjoy life at such expense of money and labor, as would be far below the average amount necessary to support his fellow men— as his reputation and remuneration increased, he would travel —what more needed he?

Two short novels, *The Stories of the Three Burglars* and *The Merry Chanter,* and a longer one, *Ardis Claverden,* were published in 1890. These three stories again demonstrate that

Stockton was more at home in the shorter medium. While
Ardis Claverden is an interesting novel, and contains some
appealing people and some remarkable descriptions of that
portion of Virginia, Amelia County, in which Stockton found
so much stimulating material, it is, as an entity, inferior to
the whimsy of *The Merry Chanter*. *Ardis Claverden* is the
story of the tangled romance of a beautful Virginia girl who
is pressed by several suitors, and, for nearly the length of the
novel, kept from the man of her choice by a series of mis-
understandings. Roger Dunworthy, the favored lover, has little to do but provide complications by his jealousy, but the
other aspirants for the hand of Ardis are keenly pictured,
deftly drawn characters. Dr. Lester, in the hopeless position
of "friend of the family," who generously takes the burden
of aiding the lovers, without ever mentioning his own hopeless suit, is one of Stockton's best-drawn, and most sympathetic
male characters. Tom Prouter, the energetic young English-
man who does not care what enterprise he engages in so long
as it keeps him moving, provides some very amusing moments. Egbert Dalrymple is a remarkably real person for all
that he is obviously a caricature, and his soulful refusal to
be shaken off is so ludicrous, yet so engaging, that we are
shocked when he commits suicide upon learning of Ardis'
marriage.

The romance of Ardis Claverden takes its measured course
up hill and down dale through snow and summer in Georgia
and Virginia in characteristic fashion. The episode of the
Chiverleys, Ardis' New York artist friends, is another of those
felicitous moments which Stockton always managed to in-
corporate somewhere in every novel. Mrs. Chiverley discovers
that by injecting a "meaning" into her husband's permanent
gallery of unsold pictures she can build up a satisfactory, if
moderate, demand for them. That he frequently disagrees
with her interpretation of his art, she, as a true Stocktonian
heroine, finds no drawback:

Mrs. Chiverley made some attempt to get her husband to work
a meaning into his pictures while he was painting them, but in

this she did not succeed. When they were finished they always appeared to her to mean something entirely different from what had been originally proposed; and she was forced to admit to herself that it would be better to let him go on in his own way, and for her to work in the purports after he had done his part. It was, indeed, as she had discovered in her own work, a very difficult thing to work up a picture to a fixed significance. It was ever so much easier to adapt the significance to the picture.

In the character of Bonetti, Stockton has given one of the earliest treatments of the "Georgia Cracker." Not too honest, lazy, preferring rather to hunt than to delve, "he had grown into the habit of allowing his philosophy to make up the deficits occasioned by his disinclination to hard and systematic work."

The Negroes, as usual in one of Stockton's novels with a Southern setting, are genuine, and their speech is realistically rendered. Of no great pretensions, *Ardis Claverden* represents a good Stockton standard; if it is sometimes slow moving, there are compensations in many richly descriptive scenes, and the unfailing good humor of Stockton's approach.

In *The Merry Chanter,* a shorter novel, Stockton returns to his *Rudder Grange* manner, and writes an infectious, farcical tale in which "Doris and I" enter the coastwise trade in a ship, the *Merry Chanter,* which represents Doris' dowry. Captain Timon Mucher, an old salt, signs as skipper, and brings his cronies, Captain Retire Garnish, Captain Jabez Teel, and Captain Cyrus Bodship, as crew. The proposed voyage is a happy junket for the old seamen, who are delighted once again to have a stout keel, even though encrusted with barnacles, under them. Taking on a ballast of stones, the ship warps from its pier, bound for Boston. Unintentionally the *Merry Chanter* takes as passengers a butcher, and Lord Crabstairs, fugitive from a debtor's prison. Delirious adventures ensue involving the butcher, Lord Crabstairs, Mrs. Bodship, and Dolor and Alwilda Tripp. Alwilda Tripp is a satirical character, who does what would presently be known as "surrealist" paintings on the walls of her house.

In the happy madness of the voyage—the barnacle-covered, stone-ballasted ship can barely wallow through the water—a variety of such episodes occur as only Stockton could have conceived. There is humor, but there is also waggish satire on the state of some members of the English peerage, in Stockton's depiction of the plight of Lord Crabstairs. He cites a news report:

Considerable interest has lately been excited with regard to the case of Lord Crabstairs, who recently succeeded, not to the estate,—for there is none,—but to the title of this ancient family. It is well known that his only inheritance was a vast mass of debts, some of which began to accumulate in the seventeenth century, and which were increased and multiplied by a long line of ancestors, so that many years ago it became impossible for any descendant of the house to pay them. In consequence of this unfortunate state of affairs, the new Lord Crabstairs became liable to arrest at the moment of his coming into the title, and to be sent to the debtor's jail, where so many of his forefathers had passed their lives.

The trip ends happily, of course, with Stockton's usual verve and dispatch when he was working with such material. The old *Merry Chanter* becomes in truth Doris' dowry, Lord Crabstairs escapes from his unhappy legacy, Alwilda Tripp finds new material for her brush, and the doughty old sea captains have one more voyage to remember, as they sit on the docks sucking their pipes and meditatively spitting into the quiet tide. *The Merry Chanter* is required reading for all who enjoy Stockton in his most mellow mood, with his "fancy" riding free.

A novelette published in the same year, *The Stories of the Three Burglars,* affords some interesting character studies, and one fine scene—that in which the three burglars are caught by means of wine into which a powerful narcotic has been placed. One senses that Stockton intended the story to be more exciting, more robust, than it is. The "stories" of the three burglars, to account for their presence in a strange house, are ingenious, but the material was slight, and the motivation ineffective.

By 1891 *Rudder Grange* had sold over forty thousand copies, *The Late Mrs. Null* over thirty thousand, and the collection of short stories, *The Lady or the Tiger?*, had sold over twenty-five thousand copies and was still an important item of the bookseller's stock. As has several times been indicated, Stockton was shrewdly aware of the value of his work, and he took advantage of public interest to issue several collections of short stories. These collections are something of a bibliographer's nightmare, because Stockton's publishers made a practice of issuing a new edition of short stories in which perhaps only one item—the title story—was different from a previously issued collection.[6] For a time Stockton seems to have been content to select stories from his earlier work to form these collections. He was working diligently on several novels, and reworking material for further adventures of the Rudder Grangers.

Apparently as a result of his own experience when he returned from his extensive trip abroad, Stockton began to write *The House of Martha* (1891). Returned from a long trip, Horace Vanderley is anxious to retail his varied experiences to the stay-at-homes, who have not enjoyed the broadening advantages of travel to remote parts of the earth. But, as he says, "My friends and acquaintances in town were glad to see me, not that they might hear what had happened to me, but that they might tell me what had happened to them." Of all his acquaintances, he finds only his aunt willing to listen, and she constantly falls asleep. Determined, however, to satisfy his desire for a hearing, Vanderley inserts an advertisement in a newspaper:

Wanted—A respectable and intelligent person, willing to devote several hours a day to listening to the recitals of a traveller, address, stating compensation expected, Oral.

6 Cf. contents of collections in the bibliography.

Out of what was probably his own rich experience in attempting to obtain competent secretaries, Stockton describes with an acutely satiric pen the difficulties the well-meaning, undemanding Vanderley experiences in finding somone who fits his modest requirements. His "listener," Chester Walkirk, a very jewel as a companion and *chargé d'affaires*, is unable, however, to fulfill routine secretarial duties. At the suggestion of his aunt, Vanderley secures the services of a "nun" from the House of Martha, a semi-cloistered organization of women who give their services for a time, but who have no permanent vows, in a religious sense. He becomes enamoured of his secretary, Sister Hagar, who is in life Sylvia Raynor, a beautiful, spirited girl. Much of the whimsical tone of the novel departs when Vanderley discovers he is in love with Sylvia, and the rest of the long narrative is concerned with a complicated love story, the threads of which are, of course, successfully untangled. If the later parts of the novel lack freshness—they are, in reality, rather dull—Stockton has done a very skillful scene in that in which Vanderley makes love to Sister Hagar by means of the travel narrative which he is dictating to her through a grille which the Mother Superior has forced him to build in his study before she will permit Sylvia to work for him. The character of the suspicious nun who accompanies and calls for Sister Hagar each day is most skillfully drawn, as anyone who has had experience with women living in religious communities will immediately recognize. In quieter mood than *The Merry Chanter*, less vital than *The Late Mrs. Null* or *Ardis Claverden*, *The House of Martha* is a love story with some delightful moments which will bring a deep-throated, sympathetic chuckle to those who realize the deft way in which Stockton has satirized common human failings.

No one but Stockton, with his long training in the depiction of the mildly insane, could have written such a novel as his next full-length story, *The Squirrel Inn*. One wonders if the word "Squirrel" had the same slangy connotation in 1891 that it possesses today. If so (and nuts were probably a staple article in the diet of squirrels in 1891) Stockton chose an admirable title for his country inn. The madness begins with Stephen Petter, an eccentric innkeeper, whose hostelry has no two rooms on the same level, and has indeed, one room, very desirable, reached only by a ladder from the outside. Among Petter's first guests were the Rockmores, of Germantown, who so impressed Peter that he will not receive guests who do not know "The Rockmores of Germantown."

When it became known that the Squirrel Inn was ready to receive guests people came from here and there; not very many of them, but among them were the Rockmores of Germantown. This large family, so it appeared to Stephen Petter, was composed of the kind of fellow-beings with whom he wished to associate. Their manners and ways seemed to him the manners and ways of the people he liked to read about, and he regarded them with admiration and respect. He soon discovered from their conversation that they were connected or acquainted with leading families in our principal Eastern cities, and it became his hope that he and his Squirrel Inn might become connected with these leading families by means of the Rockmores of Germantown.

Anyone who has met those who belong to Philadelphia's older society will recognize the fiendishly accurate picture Stockton has portrayed in this oblique fashion. For those who have not, the memorable story of the young debutante presented at the Court of the King of England, will illustrate:

"And from what part of America do you come?" the King genially asked of the sweet young thing curtsying so gracefully.
"From the Main Line, Your Majesty" she answered serenely.[7]

Such were the Rockmores of Germantown who affected the destiny of Squirrel Inn. Before the boat which is to take him to the Squirrel Inn sails, Walter Lodloe is requested by a strange, attractive woman to mind her baby. Courteously, with that fateful courtesy of all Stocktonian heroes, Lodloe

7 For the benefit of the still unenlightened, the "Main Line" is a residential suburb strung along the main line of the Pennsylvania Railroad from Philadelphia to the West. It includes Merion, Wynnewood, Bryn Mawr, Ardmore, and Wayne.

agrees. The boat sails, but no mother arrives to reclaim her child. The infant, hungry, begins to cry, and the suggestions which amused fellow passengers give the desperate man are a fertile source of hilarity.

Under such auspices does Lodloe's stay at Squirrel Inn begin. He meets Petter and the kindly, comfortable Mrs. Petter; he hears of "the Greek in the Outhouse," Mr. Tippengray, a classics scholar; he falls in love with the baby's mother, Mrs. Christie; and he aids in the romances of Lanigan Bean and Calthea Rose (delightful people) and Ida Mayberry, school teacher-nurse, and quiet Mr. Tippengray. The mad house itself, by its very construction, adds to an already complicated situation, and, when all is happily resolved, at the summer's end, Mrs. Petter suggests to Stephen that perhaps it would be better to have a proper house with a hall through the middle and the rooms alike on both sides. Petter's answer is a clear reflection of Stockton's own philosophy:

"It strikes me, Susan," said he, looking reflectively in front of him, "that our lives are very seldom built with a hall through the middle and the rooms alike on both sides. I don't think we'd like it if they were. They would be stupid and humdrum. The right sort of life should have its ups and downs, its ins and outs, its different levels, its outside stairs and its inside stairs, its balconies, windows, and roofs of different periods and different styles. This is education. These things are the advantages that our lives get from the lives of others."

The Squirrel Inn is a mellow novel written at a time when Stockton was thoroughly schooled in the narrative technique of his own peculiar concepts. It is humorous, it is at times hilarious, but more, it is warmly human and sympathetic. More than any other story of this, perhaps his most productive period, *The Squirrel Inn* has a definite philosophy and a quiet sympathy with life.[8]

In the same year that saw the publication of *The Squirrel Inn,* Stockton published a collection of short stories under the title *The Rudder Grangers Abroad.* The volume contains

[8] The present Squirrel Inn, on the Hudson, was named after Stockton's novel.

reprints of "Euphemia Among the Pelicans" (1882) and "Pomona's Daughter" (1883). The story of greatest interest, however, is "Derelict." Many romantic sea stories have been written about the central notion of a derelict, fully stocked with provisions, reached by survivors of another marine disaster. No one but Stockton would have toyed with the diverting idea of two derelicts, with a lover on each. Unable to control either vessel, the lovers tantalizingly drift within speaking distance several times, then in the night the vessels separate. Both are rescued and, after further adventures, reunited and married, to live happily ever after. There is genuine charm in the picture of Mary Phillips, the real heroine of the story, and the narrator, bellowing at each other across fifty yards of trackless ocean. Stockton's mingling of the improbable with the perfectly natural here produces a story of considerable charm.

"The Water-Devil" (1874) reprinted in the same volume is the story of an iron vessel turned into a mammoth magnet through the escape of "stored electricity" which it is carrying as its cargo. On its journey it is suddenly and mysteriously halted by the unbreakable clutch of spectral hands which throw the passengers and crew into a panic. The mystery is solved when it is discovered that the Water-Devil is the heavy Madras-Rangoon telegraph cable which has been attracted to the floating magnet above it. Most interesting moment of the "tall story" is the last paragraph, spoken by Mr. Harberry, one of the group who had heard the tale from the marine who narrated it: "I have often heard that marines are a class of men who are considered as fit subjects to tell tough stories to, but it strikes me that the time has come when the tables are beginning to be turned."

Interesting, too, is the way in which Stockton has realized the effect of the fear of the unknown upon the people on the ship which they have begun to believe is in the clutches of a water-devil; it is a study which is fully realized in the conduct of Miss Minturn, who, when she believes herself in danger, is most friendly toward the sturdy marine, but who, once danger is past, thought no more of "the humble sea-soldier who once stood between her and—nobody knew what."

"The Remarkable Wreck of the 'Thomas Hyke' " is the maddest derelict story ever written. Carrying a cargo of pig iron, the *Thomas Hyke* collides with another ship, and receives a great hole in her bow. The water enters, and the crew, save three, abandon ship. The pig iron shifts forward, sinking the ship vertically, but the great amount of air in the water-tight compartments prevents the ship from sinking more than thirty or forty feet below the surface. A storm causes the ship to toss, loosening the already weakened plates of the bow, and the cargo of pig iron chutes to the bottom of the sea. Released, the ship bobs to the surface, and the three survivors, who have lived comfortably under water for several days, are rescued by a searching party. The air of circumstantial detail with which Stockton has surrounded the story makes it at once plausible and incredible, a feat which gives his work so much of its charm.

It is not improbable that a count would reveal that Stockton wrote nearly as many stories with the sea as a background as he wrote landsmen's tales. One reason seems to be that the sea afforded greater scope for his free-running fancy. There no geographical limitations were imposed, to which, for his more critical readers, he was obliged to conform when he wrote of localities which could be calibrated in terms of miles, years, months, or latitudes.

For a reason almost identical, Stockton found his happiest expression in the short story, rather than in the novel, because in the shorter narrative he was able to produce a single effect from a single idea, imaginatively developed, and was not fettered by the necessity of accounting for all the loose ends of narrative detail consequent upon the elaborated interweavings of plot entailed in the novel.

Sedentary by force of circumstances, contented through the achievement of a long-cherished desire, Stockton lived quietly at The Holt during the years 1892, 1893, and 1894. Each winter he and Mrs. Stockton went to New York for a stay of several months, during which time they lived in hotels because, while he loved the city in winter, he could never be persuaded to purchase a city residence. But with the first loosening of the ground in early March, he returned to Convent Station, to see how the horses, the chickens, the new litter of puppies were thriving.

His income each year was, for his time, considerable, but it was quickly spent. He was not extravagant, but he was generous. If he had a shrewd knowledge of the value of his work in terms of money, it was the result of his own editorial experience, for, while he demanded top prices for his stories, he was most generous in aiding those less fortunate than he.

In the late months of 1893 he was working daily on *The Adventures of Captain Horn*. His diary records the fact that he "lost three months, twenty-three days on Captain Horn by absence in Chicago." In March 1894 he had returned from this single excursion into the West, of which no more extensive record apparently exists, and the adventures of Captain Horn and Mrs. Cliff were resumed. In the same year he was elected to membership in the Washington Association of New Jersey, as a member from Morris County. This election was a short time later the occasion of a memorable essay, "The Spirit of Washington," which he read before the society on February 22, 1895. The essay was so favorably received that the society undertook its publication in pamphlet form. Stockton was enjoying his years of ripest success. But a few crowded years of life remained, in which he reaped honor, wealth, and a sense of rich accomplishment. He accepted his fame modestly, and it served only to stimulate him to greater things. He had yet many things he wanted to do, and his fertile imagination was crowded with stories.

Chapter VII

FRANK STOCKTON was seldom interested in national affairs unless they touched him closely, and it was but infrequently that contemporary events were represented in his work. He never used fiction as a stone upon which to grind an axe. He had given evidence of his intense feeling concerning the Civil War by printing "A Northern Voice" at his own expense; during the Spanish-American War he was silent, although the hostilities provided him with material for two excellent short stories, "The Governor-General" and "The Skipper and El Capitan"; during the Philippine controversy, he suggested satirically that the simplest solution would be to sell all the natives as slaves. But none of these represented the wholeheartedness with which he aided in the passage of the International Copyright Bill. It was, of course, a very natural interest, since he was becoming internationally known, and many of his stories were being pirated abroad in translation. He invented a method of bringing the bill to the attention of his admirers by sending to the hundreds of persons who wrote for his autograph a printed slip asking them to work for the speedy passage of the bill. Its passage meant much to him personally, in additional revenue, but he was persuaded to agitate for it actively because he was convinced it would aid all writers, foreign as well as American, to get from their work the returns to which they were entitled.

His fertility of plot-invention, which sometimes seemed to wane, but never quite wholly disappeared, was rising again in the construction of a group of stories, chiefly novels, which gave his peculiar narrative skill and fanciful humor an outlet nearly as satisfactory as any they had heretofore found. The first of the new novels was *The Adventures of Captain Horn,*[1]

[1] New York (Scribner), 1895.

and its sequel, *Mrs. Cliff's Yacht*.[2] *The Adventures of Captain Horn* tells of the trials and triumphs of a group of interesting people, shipwrecked on the coast of Peru. Captain Horn; Mrs. Cliff, a widow; Edna Markham, a young school teacher; and her younger brother, Ralph, are the central characters. An ancient Inca treasure-mound, protected by an artificial lake, is accidentally discovered when Captain Horn releases the lever which controls the water. A group of desperadoes, the Rackbirds, who were planning to attack the nearly defenseless refugees, are conveniently drowned when the waters are released. Wishing to get help speedily—and also to secure the tremendous Inca treasure—Captain Horn decides to sail northward in a small boat with a few Negroes to work it, leaving the rest of the party to guard the treasure. Before leaving, however, the advisability of his marriage to Miss Markham is urged upon him not only by Cheditafa, a Negro who has been a priest in his own country, but by Mrs. Cliff. This action would secure the others' share in the treasure, and leave the new Mrs. Horn as the Captain's representative. Cheditafa performs the marriage.

The rest of the story concerns itself with the difficulties Captain Horn experiences in getting his party off the island and arranging to transport the great quantity of gold ingots in secret. Stockton's often evidenced inability to depict exciting action is very clearly revealed, despite the detail and circumstance with which he relates the adventure. At the novel's end, no one is surprised to learn that Captain Horn's reluctance to marry Edna Markham was induced by the fact that he had loved her all the time.

At two moments only does the novel show flashes of its author's real power. The first is in the description of the Negroes' request that Captain Horn marry so that they would have someone to look up to, someone to whom they "belonged," in his absence, a reading of the Negro character founded on Stockton's long experience with the southern darky. There is in Cheditafa, too, a curious, dignified re-

2 New York (Scribner), 1896.

semblance to the character of Queequeg, in *Moby Dick*. The
other picture of interest is more characteristic: the amusing
sequence when Mrs. Cliff, soon to be in possession of forty
million dollars, stops in Plainton, where of course she is unable to reveal her secret until the gold is safely stored. Her
feminine discontent at this situation rises to acute misery
when her charitable neighbors present her with a pair of
blankets to stave off the rigors of the coming winter. Stockton
cannily realized that such a woman would be unable to en-
dure such a situation, so he permits her to go to Paris with the
Markhams to await Captain Horn.

Most tales of buried treasure won through dangerous adventure are exciting, and Stockton has taken advantage of a
situation essentially interesting to make a narrative of adventure of a power which was for him unusual.

The sequel to *The Adventures of Captain Horn, Mrs.
Cliff's Yacht* (1896) is, by the standard of the adventure story,
not nearly as good. But it affords Stockton an opportunity for
the delineation of the character and actions of one of those
middle-aged women at which he was so accomplished. Mrs.
Cliff, now tremendously wealthy, is attacked by a divine discontent as she encounters difficulties in spending the income
from her share of the Inca treasure. She has calculated that
her wealth increases at the rate of two dollars an hour, so
that if she considers presenting someone with a silver watch,
for instance, it immediately occurs to her to wait a few hours
and make it a gold one. She cannot make minor repairs without making such extensive renovations that a new house
would be less trouble. She buys a horse which drives excel-
lently on the way out, but, once he is turned toward home,
becomes unmanageable in his dash to the stable. Her major
frustrations and minor despairs afford Stockton some of his
finest portraiture, and he is writing at his best when he describes the varied reactions of Mrs. Cliff's neighbors to her
new estate. The novel interestingly tells of the arrival of
Mr. Burke, the mate in the Peruvian adventure, who shows

her how to spend her money both advantageously and en-
joyably, finally persuading her to buy a yacht. But the keen
humor of the story begins to dull when Mrs. Cliff's yacht
sails, for the narrative is pretentiously adventurous without
the firm motivation of the earlier novel.

With the publication of *A Chosen Few* (1895) Stockton
again gave evidence of his habit of reissuing his popular
stories with but few variations, the same group under a new
title. *A Chosen Few,* for instance, contains "A Tale of Negative Gravity," "Asaph," "His Wife's Deceased Sister," "The
Lady, or the Tiger?" "The Remarkable Wreck of the
'Thomas Hyke,'" "Old Pipes and the Dryad," "The Transferred Ghost," "A Philosophy of Relative Existences," and "A
Piece of Red Calico." This last story, "A Piece of Red Calico,"
was apparently a favorite one, for he has printed it in five
different collections of short stories. It is a shrewd satire on
the difficulty of persuading department-store clerks that you
want what you want when you want it.

Published also in 1896 was a short book for boys and girls,
*New Jersey from the Discovery of the Scheyickbi to Recent
Times,*[3] which was reissued later in the same year by the
American Book Company as *Stories of New Jersey.* The book
is a pseudo-scholarly account of certain dramatic events in the
building of New Jersey, and, because of Stockton's long experience in writing juvenile stories, it is a picturesque history.

In February 1897 *The Critic,* a literary magazine, con-
ducted a symposium on the subject of International Arbitra-
tion between Great Britain and the United States, a matter
of national interest then, since Great Britain had refused to
arbitrate the matter of the Venezuelan boundary line, and
President Cleveland maintained that the interests of the
United States, under the Monroe Doctrine, were involved.
The Critic printed opinions from an imposing group: John
Burroughs, Richard Burton, Nicholas Murray Butler, Mary
Mapes Dodge, Edward Eggleston, Charles W. Eliot, Horace

[3] New York (D. Appleton and Co.), 1896.

Howard Furness, Richard Watson Gilder, Edward Everett Hale, Julia Ward Howe, Robert Underwood Johnson, H. E. Krehbiel, Gifford Pinchot, Moses Coit Tyler, and Frank R. Stockton. Stockton's opinion was, as usual, tempered and reasonable.

I am most heartily in favor of the arbitration treaty between this country and England, an international compact which should go into history under the title of "The Cleveland Treaty," and which marks the beginning of an advance in true civilization and enlightenment which is shown by no other event in this century. Should the senate of the United States interfere with the ratification of this treaty, it will be an additional reason for the growing belief that an "Upper House" is incompatible with the idea of a true republic.

In 1897 Lippincotts published *Captain Chap, or the Rolling Stones*. This story had originally appeared in *Golden Days* in two parts, "Philip Berkeley, or The Master's Gun" and its sequel, "Captain Chap." Lippincotts combined the stories and published them under one title; some difficulty arose in clearing title to the stories, since both Stockton and the owner of *Golden Days* claimed the rights for book publication. The matter was finally settled satisfactorily, and a new edition, with the title changed to *The Young Master of Hyson Hall*, was published in 1899.

Serial publication of *The Buccaneers and Pirates of Our Coast* began in *St. Nicholas Magazine* [4] in November 1897. The history of this antiseptic account of one of the most glamorous episodes of early American history is unusually well documented, and its inclusion here is intended to show Stockton's methods of working and to offer first-hand evidence of the reasons for the stodginess of this book, which, in the hands of another, might have been a definitive and stirring account of piracy. The book had its genesis in a letter which Miss Kate Stephens, editor of a series, *Stories from American History*, published by the Macmillan Company, wrote to Stockton early in 1897, suggesting that he write a

4 Vol. XXV (November 1897–July 1898).

history of piracy in American waters. On April 23 Stockton wrote the following letter to Mrs. Dodge: [5]

Dear Mrs. Dodge:

This is a matter of business—I have been asked by a New York publisher to write a series of stories to be issued as a book, the subject being the exploits and adventures of the celebrated pirates of the American coasts, including Captain Kidd, Blackbeard, etc. Of course the material will have to be managed in a very careful manner, the subject treated as a matter of history, and the wickedness and the adventure each kept in its proper place. I think you know my style of doing that sort of thing. It has been thought advisable to publish the matter as a serial before book publication, and that is the reason I write to you. I would like you to consider my proposition solely from your own point of view, for I have not yet made up my mind whether, or not, I shall write the book at all.

Before deciding I should like to ask you these questions:

1. Would you care to have a serial on this subject from 50,000 to 60,000 words in length?

2. If you should take this series could you finish the publication of it by July, 1898? Manuscript to be furnished about October 1st, 1897.

3. Would you be willing to pay $2000 for the serial rights?

This matter is not of especial importance to me as I have not decided to do the work. I only promised to see what arrangement could be made in regard to a serial publication before I entered upon a definite consideration of the proposition.

As this is a confidential letter it has been written by my High-Confidential Secretary, who joins with me in hoping that you are well, and enjoying this beautiful Spring weather.

Sincerely yours,
Frank R. Stockton

Mrs. Dodge apparently expressed interest, for Stockton wrote to her while on a trip to Washington:

---

[5] I am indebted to Mrs. J. M. Dodge, of Philadelphia, and her son, Mr. Kern Dodge, for this group of Stockton letters and others which I have quoted from time to time.

1607–16th Street
Washington, D. C.,
May 17th, 1897.

Dear Mrs. Dodge,

Since I received your letter I have had further advantageous propositions from the publishing house which asked me to write the series of "Stories of American Pirates," (or some other title of that sort) and I have concluded to undertake the work. I will say confidentially that the book will be published by the Macmillan Company. . . .

I shall begin writing the sketches early in June. They will not all be separate and distinct stories because some of the subjects demand a more extended treatment than need be given to others; but the stories will be so arranged that it can be easily divided into installments of five thousand words,—more or less. These sketches will be founded upon historical facts and legends, but they will be told as stories.

In answer to your proposition to pay $1000, for half the series, I will say that the price at which I offered you the whole series was very low; not half of what I generally charge for that amount of material; but in this case it would satisfy me, when considered in connection with the terms for the publication of the book. But if I sell half of it at $1000, I am obliged to lose the other thousand, or else place half the stories in other periodicals, which I do not think would be desirable in any way. But I will make another proposition. Suppose St. Nicholas pays me $1500, and receives therefor the right of using just as much of the series as you want, provided it is printed before July, 1898. If you wish, some of the early papers could be furnished in September, (or sooner), and I expect to finish the whole series in November. Thus you would have the option of using what you chose, and you might like some of the sketches in the latter half better than some of those in the first part. I think this price will be considered reasonable, even if you use only half the material.

Mrs. Dodge agreed to his terms, and Stockton's next letter discusses details of publication.

Convent Station,
Morris Co., N. J.
June 5, 1897.

My dear Mrs. Dodge:—

I have been away from home for several weeks and have had so much to do since I returned that I have been delayed in answering your last letter. But I will say, in general, that everything in it is entirely to my mind and I think we shall go on very pleasantly together with our pirates. There is a good deal of research necessary before I can begin this series of sketches, but I hope very soon to start out in actual work upon it. I may not be able to put all of it into your hands by August 15th, but I can give you enough to begin with—say material for two or three months. I wish to arrange the matter so that each installment will be, in a measure, complete in itself, although there will be a general connection so that they will appear properly, as a whole, in the book. I have no doubt that if you finish the series in the July number for 1898, (which appears in June), there will be no difficulty on that score. But I have agreed that no serial by me, excepting one which is to be printed in Harper's Weekly, shall appear in the latter half of 1898. So if you begin the series in the November issue for 1897, you will be able to use a good many installments before July, 1898.

As for the title, we can easily arrange that, as the title for the series need not be the same as that of the book. As soon as I can I will prepare some titles which I will submit to you. Perhaps we may get "Buccaneers" into the title. That does not sound quite so blood-thirsty as "pirates," or perhaps we could use one of those which you suggest, such as "Stories of the High Seas." But we will get up a lot of titles to choose from.

As for the character of the sketches, we would not want pirates-and-water, for that would be too thin a mixture; but we will serve up our robbers with sugar and cream which will conceal whatever is disagreeable in their flavor. I want to make these sketches stirring and lively, infusing as much fun into the adventures as circumstances will permit.

During these weeks Stockton was busily studying the history of piracy, chiefly as told by the leading authority on the subject, John Esquemeling, whose *Buccaneers of Amer-*

ica he later mentions. As his knowledge of the subject grew, his suggestions, particularly for the title, underwent constant modification.

Convent Station,
Morris Co.,
July 16th, 1897.

Dear Mrs. Dodge,

I intended sooner to write to you in regard to the title of our proposed piratical enterprise, but I have been prevented. How would you like
"The Sea-Robbers of Our Coast"?
This would cover the ground, strike the key-note of adventure, and yet be inoffensive to those who would not associate with pirates, knowing them to be such. I will remind you that the title of the serial papers need not be that of the book. I have an idea that the Macmillans will want a straight-out pirate title, but St. Nicholas can have whatever he likes.

I am at work on the papers, and although I shall not be able to give you the whole of the manuscript by August 15th, I can give you enough of it for the artist to begin on. The installments (most of them) may be considered complete in themselves, or not, just as you please.

Convent Station
Morris Co., N. J.
July 27, 1897.

Dear Mrs. Dodge:—

On our return from our little "outing" I received your letter, and am very glad indeed to hear that you are better . . . How would you like "The Buccaneers of our Coast" as a title? Most of the pirates of the period of which I treat were buccaneers. I use the words "our coast" because many parties of Buccaneers crossed the isthmus and had their adventures down the west coast of South America, and these exploits will not come within the scope of my sketches. The first part of the series is, in a manner, historical, because I wish to make this great system of piracy clearly understood by my readers. I will send you a batch of it as soon as it is properly corrected and prepared.

With best wishes to all of you from all of us,

Sincerely yours,

Frank R. Stockton

Convent Station
Morris Co., N. J.
August 11, 1897.

My dear Mrs. Dodge:—

I sent to-day, by express, to the office, fifteen chapters of the "pirate papers,"—in the neighborhood of 30,000 words. I shall be glad to have you use whatever pleases you, and if you wish to omit a chapter, a paragraph, a sentence or a word please do so without hesitation. I do not think you will want to use all I have written in the latest chapters concerning L'Olonnois—perhaps you may not want to use him at all. He was an interesting but brutal figure.

I shall very soon send you another batch, though not so large as this, so your artists will have plenty of opportunity for the selection of subjects. I think a great many striking pictures can be made and if the artists want authentic portraits of some of the buccaneers they can find them at the Astor library, in an old book, "The Buccaneers of America," by John Esquemeling.

I enclose some suggestions for your announcement, to be added to or subtracted from, as much as you please.

Mrs. Dodge has written on the corner of this letter, "Eighteen formidable suggestions." As late as mid-September, Stockton was still undecided about the title of the series, chiefly because, since he was still writing it, he was still learning about pirates and their unpredictable ways. The last letter illuminates this point.

Convent Station
Morris Co., N. J.
Sept. 9, 1897.

My dear Mrs. Dodge:—

I write in haste to say that I am reading the proof of the pirate sketches and that I have suggested a change in the title. "The

Buccaneers of Our Coast," is a misnomer in various ways, and this I did not comprehend when I suggested it. Many of the later sketches concern men who were not buccaneers at all, but *pirates,* and very interesting ones, such as Blackbeard and Captain Kidd. I therefore propose the title "The Sea-Robbers of America." The latter part of this is also an improvement, for the West Indies are not really a part of our coast. Next week I expect to send manuscript, *largely.*

The Buccaneers and Pirates of Our Coasts (as the book was finally published in 1898) is not a very satisfactory account of the roaring days of freebooters along the Southern Coast, the Gulf, and the West Indies. The episodes are comprehensive enough, but Stockton was seemingly too aware of the morals of the audience for which he was writing. The result is an emasculated account of famous pirates not nearly as thrilling as the chief source from which Stockton took his material, Esquemeling. Kate Stephens, who suggested the series to Stockton, has written of her disappointment when she saw Stockton's manuscript:

He wrote the book [*The Buccaneers and Pirates of Our Coasts*] at my suggestion, when I was editing the *Stories from American History* series for the Macmillan Company. After reading the manuscript, and getting others' opinions upon it, I had to tell him (and with regret) that we did not find the book so gladsome, bright and inviting as we had wished it to be—in fact he seemed to have written down his subject. And I asked him to make certain changes.

He answered in great seriousness, lines of his mouth drawing in, that he could not make the subject captivating, their life admirable. Of course he meant *morally* he could not. That was understood at the time.

When I thought of the subject as one for a book for the series, it seemed to me that Mr. Stockton was the ideal author to write the book, and now the manuscript before [me] lacked the sparkle, the verve, the humor his writings commonly had. Naturally I was disappointed in the fruit of his labors, and disappointed in not getting a rouser for the series.[6]

6 Letter to Prof. W. L. Werner, dated Nov. 24, 1923.

The book, while not scholarly, is by no means lacking in authority; its chief defect was Stockton's moral inability to write anything which would glorify, or englamour, a subject intrinsically wicked. No more than Dante could have written *The Decameron,* or Saint Augustine could have written *Thus Spake Zarathustra,* could Stockton bring himself to describe with "sparkle, verve and humor" the deeds of Blackbeard, Lafitte, and Kidd. Neither would he preach moral homilies on them. But if one great criterion of a book is its appeal, then the fact that copies of *The Buccaneers and Pirates of Our Coasts* appear on the shelves of the children's room of nearly every library should be an index of its enduring interest, through intrinsic interest of subject, if not of style or color.

During the middle years of the nineties the Stocktons had made increasingly frequent trips to Washington, and the Capital had attracted them for longer and longer stays, although from each trip Stockton was delighted to get back to his Convent Station home, The Holt. During a long stay at 1607 16th Street, Washington, Stockton wrote one of his most delightful burlesques. It was inspired by one of the musical-comedy episodes of the Spanish-American War, and by the well-known indifference of certain provincial governors as to which flag flew over their consulates, so long as their tropical comfort was not disturbed. "The Governor-General"[7] tells of Señor Gonzales Proventura y Torado, of the island of Mañana, who is inventing a new chromatic scale in which all the desired combinations of color are to be furnished by parrots. But, at the moment, the Governor is out of gunpowder. The arrival of a Cabotian man-of-war is the first intimation the Governor receives that his country is at war with Cabotia. He confesses his lack of powder, and courteously is given a barrel so that he can at least fire a few shots in defense of his island. The powder is nearly used, and the Governor, realizing that he will not be able to shoot the parrots necessary for the completion of his chromatic scale

7 *Cosmopolitan,* Vol. XXV (October 1898), pp. 677.

unless some is saved, surrenders. By means open only to those reared in the Hidalgo tradition, the Governor-General and the Captain of the Cabotian ship arrange that everything shall go on as before, with the Governor-General as a brevet-citizen of Cabotia in command, and the citizens will be supplied with food, clothing, and gunpowder by the man-of-war. The ship steams away, leaving Mañana under a new flag, considerably richer than ever before. The man-of-war never returned, the supplies were consumed, and the Governor-General, seated disconsolately on a rock, gazing over the empty sea, sighed that there were no other worlds to conquer him.

The tone of high moral purpose, combined with a recognition of practical considerations, makes the story a shrewd commentary upon the permanence of high moral principles when immediate considerations are more appealing. "The Governor-General" is high comedy, in the best tradition of comedy. It was based upon an actual incident of the Spanish-American War, in which an American warship called at Guam, and had its hostile shots mistaken for a salute by the Governor, who apologized for not returning it because of a shortage of ammunition.

In 1898 Stockton published four volumes, *What Might Have been Expected*,[8] published in *St. Nicholas* in 1873-74, *The Great Stone of Sardis*,[9] *The Buccaneers and Pirates of Our Coasts*,[10] and *The Girl at Cobhurst*.[11] The scene of *The Girl at Cobhurst* is laid in a country village, to which come Ralph Haverly and his sister, Miriam, to take up residence at Cobhurst, an estate which they have inherited. The cross-currents created by the endeavors of Miss Panney, a plain-spoken, match-making old maid, to engage the affections of Ralph to Dora Bannister, a well-to-do young woman of the village, and the simultaneous efforts of La Fleur, the most gifted of cooks, to settle his affections upon her one-time mis-

8 New York (Dodd, Mead), 1898.
9 New York (Harper), 1898.
10 New York (Macmillan), 1898.
11 New York (Scribner), 1898.

tress, Cecily Drane, constitute the action of the novel. For its length, *The Girl at Cobhurst*, is slow moving and insufficiently motivated. The machinations of the female characters occupy hundreds of pages of description, and we are relieved, rather than glad, when Ralph finally succumbs to Cecily Drane. Miss Panney is one of Stockton's effective spinsters, but she is dwarfed by the excellent La Fleur, who wields, through her high culinary art, an astonishing influence—for, as Stockton remarks, "we are all slaves of our cooks, and all we can do is try and be the slaves of a good one." *The Girl at Cobhurst* is not in Stockton's better manner. We cannot become interested in the people—except the benevolent La Fleur—and consequently the action, slow at best, is uninteresting. Of much better quality, and more characteristic, was his next long story, *The Associate Hermits.*[12]

The Associate Hermits is an amusing satire on the fateful results of the unfettered exercise of individuality. Stockton gently satirizes those who would flout conventional behavior. Mr. and Mrs. Archibald are persuaded by their daughter to take the honeymoon trip in her place, leaving the bride and groom at home to begin their married life amid comfortable and familiar surroundings. The incident was founded upon an actual situation which Stockton himself suggested to the bride-to-be. Stockton takes the Archibalds to a *de luxe* camp and assembles a group of potential individualists in a woodland setting. There is, of course, the usual Stocktonian romance with several lovers pursuing one beloved. Into this not-too-idyllic fastness he introduces the Bishop, whose philosophic indefiniteness is shared by too many of one's acquaintances for his character to have been created altogether from imagination. The nub of the satire is reached in the person of Mrs. Perkenpine, camp cook, whose sudden discovery of the joys of individuality interferes seriously with the internal economy of the "paying" individualists. Her discovery is epochal. Matlock, a guide, finds Mrs. Perkenpine trying to make herself comfortable:

12 New York (Harper), 1899.

"I'll tell you what it is, Mrs. Perkenpine," he said, "you'll get yourself into the worst kind of a hole if you go off this way, leavin' everything at sixes and sevens behind you."

"It's my nater," said she. "I'm findin' it out and gittin' it ready to show to other people. You're the fust one that's seed it. How do you like it?"

"I don't like it at all," said the guide, "and I have just come to tell you that if you don't go back to your tent and cook supper to-night and attend to your business, I'll walk over to Sadler's and tell Peter to send some one in your place. I'm goin' over there anyway, if he don't send a man to take Martin's place."

"Peter Sadler!" ejaculated Mrs. Perkenpine, letting her tumbled newspaper fall into her lap. "He's a man that knows his own nater, and lets other people see it. He lives his own life, if anybody does. He's individdle down to the heels, and just look at him! He's the same as a king. I tell you, Phil Matlock, that the more I knows myself, just me, the more I'm tickled. It seems like scootin' round in the woods, findin' all sorts of funny hoppin' things and flowers that you never seed before. Why, it 'ain't been a whole day since I begun knowin' myself, and I've found out lots. I used to think that I liked to cook and clean up, but I don't; I hate it."

The culinary department finally has its mind restored to its old unquestioning serenity; the proper lovers are united, but the poor Bishop's indefiniteness has waylaid him into becoming the fiancé of Miss Raybold, whose incessantly vocal theorizing on man and nature bode not well for his future peace. Again, by introducing fine people under unusual circumstances, Stockton has triumphed over the slim material afforded by his central idea—and once again he has cut a female figure, Mrs. Perkenpine, indelibly on the mind of his reader.

From March 21 to April 28, *Literature,* then a thriving journal of letters, conducted a voting contest for the establishment of outstanding writers as candidates for an American Academy, on lines similar to the French Academy. In the final tally, Stockton was voted fifth place, being preceded by William Dean Howells, John Fiske, Mark Twain, and Thomas

Bailey Aldrich. Henry James was sixth, S. Weir Mitchell seventh, and Bret Harte eighth. For students of this rich period of American literature the choices are most interesting. That Howells should be in first place and Mark Twain in third place, after John Fiske, may surprise those whose understanding of the period is superficial. Stockton's selection over Henry James, S. Weir Mitchell, and Bret Harte is evidence of the secure niche he had carved for himself in the affections of an extensive audience.

In July 1899 Stockton moved again, for the last time. His frequent trips to Virginia, to Washington, to West Virginia, had familiarized him with the beauty of the region, and he had purchased a magnificent home, Claymont, near Charles Town, West Virginia. He sold The Holt for $30,000, and moved his possessions and his gardener, Joseph, to his new home in the Shenandoah Valley. The land on which Claymont was built was originally owned by George Washington, and the house was built by Bushrod Washington from plans drawn by George Washington himself. Claymont was built in 1820, but the house which Stockton occupied was a building which replaced the original, which had been destroyed by fire about 1837. Here, on a scale even more grand than that permitted at The Holt, Stockton was pleased to play one double rôle which he had always desired, that of the successful author and the gentleman farmer. He settled into his new life quickly, and finished a new novel, *A Bicycle of Cathay*.

A Bicycle of Cathay,[13] not quite as fine a title as he had originally intended,[14] concerns a series of mild and unfinished flirtations, rather tentatively conducted by a young gentleman setting out for his vacation on a bicycle. This young man's fancy was ripe for thoughts of love, and when a series of mishaps to attractive girls along the road place him in the position of rescuer, he allows the charms of each to engage his thoughts. An attractive six-foot young man has always points

13 New York (Harper), 1900.
14 Originally, *A Cycle of Cathay*, but W. A. P. Martin had published (1899) an historical work on China under that title. To avoid confusion, Stockton changed the title of his novel to *A Bicycle of Cathay*.

of interest for the nubile female, wherever else her affections may be engaged, and it surprises no one but the young tourist that their interest in him goes no deeper than friendship, and that they all marry quite suitably elsewhere. He himself marries the doctor's daughter in his own town, proving thereby once again that the longest way round is sometimes the shortest way home. *A Bicycle of Cathay* has a placid charm, and in its heroines gives unusually fresh pictures of young womanhood. The quality of the picaresque which it possesses is slight, however, since so many of the adventures are trivial, and the character of the young bicyclist is fundamentally not very interesting. The chief value of the novel lies in Stockton's unexpected drawing of a young woman of vitality and appeal. He was not often so successful with women under forty.

One of Stockton's best collections of short stories was published in 1900 under the title *Afield and Afloat*.[15] A genial introduction loosely integrates the stories, but each in its way is noteworthy. The first story is "The Buller-Podington Compact," [16] which has suggested the title of the collection. "The Buller-Podington Compact" tells of two friends "who find that while there is joy afield and happiness afloat, it is dangerous to forsake a chosen element and to do that which may give an amphibious nature to one's experiences. The two friends . . . are not the first to find out that a mixture of land and water makes mud." Buller and Podington, business partners and fast friends, have for years avoided visiting each other's summer homes. Buller was fond of boating, which Podington hated; Podington was fond of driving spirited horses, which frightened Buller. They make a compact to visit each other—Buller to ride with Podington, and Podington to sail with Buller. Quite naturally, in a short story by Stockton, the two diversions are hilariously combined, the Podington trip becoming semi-aquatic and the Buller sail taking place chiefly under horse power. These

---

15 New York (Scribner), 1900.
16 *Scribner's Magazine* Vol. XXII (August 1897), p. 217.

situations are in themselves humorous, but the story rises to a finer level in the characterization of the friends' grim courage, deftly understated, in undergoing precisely the ex$_t$erience which each has most dreaded. Additional charm is given the story, too, by Stockton's depiction of the way in which each rises to his specialty in the emergency. Thus Buller, the sailor, extricates them from the episode of the submerged carriage, while Podington, the horseman, successfully prevents tragedy in the episode of the boating trip.

"The Romance of a Mule Car" [17] is a tale of two lovers, seeking privacy so that he can propose to her, who find it finally in the deserted interior of a mule-car, which is soon to be replaced by a shiny electric trolley, because "the people here now have no use for mule-cars."

"The Governor-General" [18] is included in the collection, as is another story inspired by the Spanish-American War, "The Skipper and El Capitan." [19] Ezra Budrack, skipper of the *Molly Crenshaw,* carries his wife and his pretty daughter with him on his voyaging. He is a friend of Matias Romino, El Capitan, whose ship, the *Reina de la Plata,* is met at Yakonsk, a Russian trading station in Alaska. The romance between Drusilla and El Capitan is about to reach its climax when the startled captains learn of the war between their countries. The Russian commandant insists that it is their duty to put to sea and fight. Woefully the men agree. Yankee ingenuity triumphs over Castilian guile, and the *Reina de la Plata* becomes Skipper Budrack's prize. International law, however, will allow only one vessel at a time to enter the neutral Russian harbor, so the *Molly Crenshaw* sails on a trading expedition while the *Reina* is being repaired. When Budrack returns, he learns that his wife and daughter have sailed with El Capitan in search of him, and that he must remain in port for twenty-four hours after the *Reina* has left. The Skipper finds matters at a sorry pass, so he goes off philosophically to breakfast with the Russian commandant. Then

17 *Century Magazine,* Vol. XXXIII (November 1897), p. 127.
18 *Cosmopolitan,* Vol. XXV (October 1898), p. 677.
19 *Cosmopolitan,* Vol. XXVI (November 1898), p. 84.

the *Reina* comes steaming serenely into port, bearing the news that the war is over. El Capitan announces his engagement to Drusilla, and the Skipper arranges to buy the *Reina de la Plata* as a wedding present for his daughter and his new son-in-law. The story has that quaint flavor of the absurdly logical which was one of Stockton's great contributions to the American short story.

Stockton undertook but once to essay the tale of ratiocination, and he approaches the murder mystery in characteristic fashion. In "Struck by a Boomerang," he tells of the strange murder of Reuben Farris, and of the way in which the narrator sets out logically to detect the murderer, only to prove, by incontrovertible evidence, that he himself is the guilty one. He is saved by the timely confession of the true murderer. The story is the expression of one of Stockton's little truths, that circumstances frequently are misleading. The concluding paragraph has a wider application than its relation to the story:

I have had very good success in the law, but for some years I never pressed an investigation, never endeavored to find out the origin of some evil action, without stopping to consider whether it might not be possible that under some peculiar circumstances, and in some way I did not understand at the time, I might not be the man I was looking for, and that the legal blow I was about to deliver might not be turned, boomerang-like, upon my astonished self.

"Come In, New Year" and "A Sailor's Knot," contained in the same volume, are pleasant love stories. The best story in *Afield and Afloat,* however—indeed one of Stockton's finest—is "The Great Staircase at Landover Hall." [20] Begun as a routine Christmas story, and using a familiar spectral motive, Stockton has so combined the elements as to make a new tale, somewhat sentimental perhaps, but written with restraint and charm. A wealthy young man discovers a fine old house, furnished with rich and beautiful things, which he admires so much that he immediately buys it. Alone on

[20] *Harper's Weekly,* December 17, 1898.

Christmas Eve, the new owner of Landover Hall sits quietly smoking before the great fireplace. The clock on the landing of the staircase strikes twelve, and with the last stroke, he sees descending the stairs a beautiful young woman dressed in an olden fashion. It is the spirit of Evelyn Heatherton, first mistress of the house, whose portrait hangs on the wall of the hallway. The narrator speaks to her, falls in love with her quiet beauty. The spell is broken by the crash of the clock striking one. The narrator learns that descendents of Evelyn Heatherton live in the same town, and out of chivalry and curiosity he calls on old Mrs. Heatherton, granddaughter of the woman who had visited him at midnight. There he meets Mrs. Heatherton's daughter, the image, in flesh and blood, of the Evelyn with whom he had fallen hopelessly in love. Her name, also, is Evelyn, and matrimonial matters of a less spectral nature are speedily arranged. The following Christmas Eve, the vision of the first Evelyn returns to make welcome the new mistress of Landover Hall. "The Great Staircase at Landover Hall" is one of those fragile stories on a familiar theme, which lose their charm, their fragrance, when reduced to the narrative elements alone. Stockton proves that while graciousness may be a thing of the past, it can be a thing of the present as well.

The concluding story in the collection is one of Stockton's maddest adventures. "A Landsman's Tale" introduces the preposterous notion of a landlubber presuming to tell a story of shipwreck to a group of New England deep-water men. They listen, open-mouthed, while the narrator describes the literary proclivities of a ship's crew. As the ship was foundering, and the captain was deciding what to take with them in the open boats, the first mate spoke for the others:

"Captain," said he, "we have made up our minds. If it is only forty-five miles to the nearest land, we can easily row that far without eating. When we reach the island, even if it should be a desert one, it is not unlikely that we shall find some sort of food, berries, birds, or bread-fruit, and almost certainly some fish in the adjacent water, but there is no reason to suppose that upon such islands we shall find books. Therefore, we have unanimously agreed that we will take with us our library. There's not a man among us who is not interested in a story or in a historical volume, and to leave our books behind would be a wrench, Captain, which in all deference to your opinion, if it be otherwise, we truly think we ought not be obliged to give ourselves."

In a faltering voice the Captain spoke:

"My men," said he, "you have chosen wisely; I will lower the library to the boat."

The narrator, noting that "on the face of every captain there seemed to be a shadow which grew darker and darker as grows the sky before a storm," discreetly takes his leave. The satire seems originally to have been inspired by a society which collects books to be placed in the crew's quarters of ships habitually taking long voyages. It is easy to perceive how Stockton's ready fancy would take such an idea, embroider it to the point of absurdity, and produce a waggish, if inoffensive, satire.

During 1901 Stockton spent most of his time at his new home, supervising minor improvements in the fine old house and restoring the tangled gardens to their former prim beauty. He was writing also, daily dictating 1,500 words of *The Captain's Toll Gate*,[21] a story which was destined not to be published until after his death.

The Captain's Toll Gate is another of Stockton's mellow surveys of the ways of three men and a maid. Olive Asher, an attractive girl of twenty, lives with her uncle, Captain Asher, during her father's naval voyages. When she learns that her father is to marry one of her own schoolmates, she makes up her mind immediately to marry, and so make herself independent of his household. As her affections are not engaged by any of the three young men who pay suit to her she keeps them dangling in a most matter-of-fact fashion. A slight misunderstanding with her uncle, brought about by an unpleasant female, Maria Port, who has matrimonial designs upon him, is cleared up and, since the immediate necessity for a

21 New York (Appleton), 1903.

marriage disappears, she dismisses her suitors and goes on a trip with Captain Asher. In Washington, Captain Asher frustrates an attempted assassination, and would himself have fallen victim to the thwarted murderer had not Olive seized the man's pistol and dispatched him. Her quick-thinking brings on much undesirable publicity, but also brings the fourth and most desirable suitor, Dick Lancaster, to declare his love. Captain Asher's appeal to the village Dorcas Society rouses these worthy women to rout the still pursuing Maria Port, and the romance ends happily with the marriage of Olive and Dick. The slow pace of the novel detracts considerably from its interest, and Olive's disinclination toward any of her suitors makes the recitation of their wooing uninteresting. The figure of greatest interest in the novel is that of the least pleasant character, Maria Port. She is the perfect picture of the acidulous, determined female. Even her description, when first we meet her, is ominous:

> This was a middle-aged woman, dressed in black holding a black fan. She wore a black bonnet with a little bit of red in it. Her face was small and pale, its texture and color suggesting a boiled apple dumpling. She had small eyes of which it can be said that they were of a different color from her face, and were therefore noticeable. Her lips were not prominent, and were closely pressed together as if someone had begun to cut a dumpling, but had stopped after making one incision.

Maria Port is indeed a formidable woman, but our interest in her machinations rises only to tepidity.

Before *The Captain's Toll Gate* was quite finished, the Appleton Company requested Stockton to write a pirate romance based on the sort of adventures he had retailed in *The Buccaneers and Pirates of Our Coasts*. The result was *Kate Bonnet, the Romance of a Pirate's Daughter*. *Kate Bonnet* is a vigorous story of derring-do on the Spanish Main, and is complete evidence that Stockton was not at home in the medium of the straight adventure narrative, despite the fact that structurally *Kate Bonnet* is one of his most carefully constructed plots. Stripped of its complications, *Kate Bonnet* tells of the determination of Major Stede Bonnet to become a pirate. He outfits a vessel, ships a piratical crew and, taking his daughter aboard, plunges the narrative into a welter of well-diluted blood, and into the midst of a group of musical-comedy pirates of whom Blackbeard is the most notable. Stockton has attempted to give a seventeenth-century flavor by meticulously calling his characters "Mistress Kate," "Master Martin Newcombe," "Dame Bonnet," by introducing sword play and boarding parties, resounding oaths and pannikins of rum—but the effort is not successful. Additional evidence that it was not successful is attested by the almost universal bewilderment of the critics who first reviewed the book. Most of them, in America as well as abroad, did not understand it. In view of Stockton's previous novels, it marked a clear departure, and they were unwilling to believe that he had not written it as a satire on adventure stories or as burlesque on "the pirate bold" or, most unusual conjecture of all, that Stockton was deliberately, with a solemn face, writing a story so that he could laugh at his readers.

Stockton was more distressed by the reception which *Kate Bonnet* received than by anything which had been said of his work before. Shortly after the book's publication he went to Atlantic City for a month, and upon his return to his winter quarters in New York wrote the following letter to the Boston *Times,* March 23, 1902:

I have been prevented by absence from home from sooner acknowledging the very admirable and cheering review of my book, *Kate Bonnet,* which recently appeared in your journal. I experienced a peculiar pleasure in reading this review from the fact that its author did not imagine that my book was a *satire* on historical fiction, or that it was meant to be anything else but a straightforward story of some men and women who lived in the early part of the eighteenth century, and who disported themselves according to their various natures. I shall be obliged if you will present my earnest thanks to your reviewer.

Stockton remained about two weeks longer in New York, then went South, intending to return to Charles Town and

Claymont, after a short stay in Washington. He attended the banquet of the National Academy of Sciences, at which he was a guest, on Wednesday, April 16, 1902. He was taken ill at the banquet, and was carried to his room in the Willard Hotel, where he died of a cerebral hemorrhage, on April 20. His body was shipped to the home of his sister, Louise Stockton, at 4213 Chester Avenue, Philadelphia. The funeral was attended by his friends in great numbers. Mark Twain came, as did Richard Watson Gilder, A. B. Frost, James Meade Dodge, Charles Collins, the publisher, J. Herbert Morse, the editor, his old associate, George Cary Eggleston, accompanied by a committee from the Authors Club. He was buried in Woodlands Cemetery, in a plot overlooking the Schuylkill River, not a half-mile from the place where he was born. The story-teller's story ended on the same quiet note that he had himself so often used.

Before his death, Stockton had been engaged in arranging a collection of short stories. Inventing a mythical garden, and a gardener, John Gayther, Stockton gathers a group of friends who tell the stories. *John Gayther's Garden and the Stories Told Therein* was published posthumously, Mrs. Stockton herself completing the links in the last few stories. The "John Gayther" arrangement was simply a device to give the volume a certain unity, although the stories are gathered from his better stories of the past two years.

"What I Found in the Sea" [22] tells of Gayther's discovery of a Spanish galleon and an English ship. Descending for treasure, in a diver's suit, Gayther finds that an enemy has cut the air pipe. He discovers a row of empty casks, inserts the severed tube therein, and manages to breathe until he can free himself of his clumsy suit. Having "breathed the air of the sixteenth century," he swears atmospherically upon his return to the boat, confounds his enemy, and amazes his friends. The treasure, of course, is never rediscovered. The tale is a Stocktonian "tall story," told with disarming effrontery. Of better quality and of deeper interest is "The Lady

[22] *Cosmopolitan*, Vol. XXVII (June 1899).

in the Box," [23] a story of a woman preserved for forty years in a state of trance such that her youthful beauty never fades. A foreign setting aids in preserving an air of romantic credibility, and the chief interest of the story is cleverly focused on her awakening. "The Cot and the Rill" [24] is a tale somewhat in the *Rudder Grange* manner, telling of the wife of a millionaire who seeks the simpler things of life, and finds a cot on a rill which suits her ideas of the rustic. Her indulgent husband buys the countryside for miles around, transforms the cot and the rill into a miracle of rusticity *de luxe*. Some rather ingenious details are worked into the story, but the tone is so decidedly that of burlesque that the humor is often strained, and the development of the incident over-elaborate. "My Balloon Hunt" [25] is another "tall story" in which a balloon is used in a tiger hunt. The balloon car swings low over the desert, the tiger leaps into the car as the hunter leaps to the ground, leaving his beloved, Irene, twenty feet in the air, in the basket with the tiger. Desperate, the hunter grasps the trailing guide rope, wades into a convenient river so that Irene can jump. She dives successfully, and the balloon is released, carrying a very frightened tiger. The story reveals Stockton's flair for turning the tables on a situation, and developing absurdity from what would otherwise be hackneyed narrative.

A benevolent ghost story, in Stockton's more sentimental manner, "The Conscious Amanda," [26] and "My Translataphone," [27] a humorous love story in the mood of "A Tale of Negative Gravity," afford a last picture of two interesting aspects of Stockton's work. "The Vice-Consort," [28] an amusing and perspicacious study of woman, is the story of how one woman, considered plain, is asked by fellow villagers to become their successor in the event of death, and of how

[23] *Cosmopolitan,* Vol. XXVII (October 1899), p. 625.

[24] *Cosmopolitan,* Vol. XXVIII (December 1899), p. 209.

[25] *Ladies' Home Journal,* Vol. XIX (March 1902), p. 56.

[26] *Cosmopolitan,* Vol. XXIX (June 1900), p. 185.

[27] *Harper's Bazaar,* Vol. XXXIII (October 27–November 3, 1900), pp. 1612, 1678.

[28] *Scribners,* Vol. XXVIII (December 1900), p. 642.

quickly they change their opinions when they discover she is engaged. "The Foreign Prince and the Hermit's Daughter" marks the last appearance of old friends—Euphemia and her husband, Pomona and Jonas. The note of finality is sounded by Pomona:

"We've been told, sir, that some editors have been asking you to get us to enter fiction again; and what we want to say is that we don't want to enter it no more. What we did when we was in it was all very well, but that's past and gone, although I've said to Jone a good many more times than once that if I had to do this or that thing now, that's set down in the book, I'd do it different. But then he always answers that if I'd done that I'd have spoiled the story, and so there was no more to say on that subject. What we've done we gladly did, and we're more than glad we did it for you, sir. But as for doing it again, we can't do it, for it ain't in us. Even if we tried to do the best we could for you, all you'd get would be something like skim-milk—good enough for cottage cheese and bonnyclabber, but nothing like good fresh milk with the cream on it."

Thus Stockton disposes of the Pomona stories, shrewdly realizing that Pomona was a mine which could not be forever worked.

The story which Pomona and Jonas tell is a fanciful tale in the best manner of *The Floating Prince* stories, and the narrative is brightened by two significant statements, both illustrative of Stockton's philosophy of composition.

"There's two ways of ending a story," said Pomona. "One is to wind it up, and the other is to let it run down—I don't mean to wind it up like a clock, but to wind it up like an old fashioned clothes-line which isn't wanted again until you have some more things to hang on it."

This was precisely the method Stockton so frequently followed. A great body of his stories "wind up"; many simply "run down," once the incident which gave them birth has been told, for Stockton had little sense of the dramatic. Some, like the *Rudder Grange* and, later, the Pomona stories, were merely wound up "like clothes-line," until he had some more things to hang on it. The characters were there, the mood was the same, but much of the charm and much of the novelty upon which their effectiveness depended was gone.

Later, Jonas quotes Stockton's opinion about writing stories with a moral:

"My opinion about morals to stories is that people who read them ought to work them out for themselves," said he. "Some people work out one kind of a moral, and others work out another kind. It was a pretty big job to write that story, which I had to do the most of and I don't think I ought to be called on to put in any moral, which is a good deal like being asked to make bread for the man who buys my wheat."

Stockton had always been disappointed when readers sought a moral in stories devoid of purpose other than entertainment, and he was equally disappointed that adults did not fully appreciate that his fairy stories and "fanciful tales" were written for the maturest appreciation, because only the mature could understand his implied commentary on life.

With *John Gayther's Garden* Frank Stockton's work came to an end. His life had been a long life and, as far as external judgments go, it had been a happy one. Certainly he had, more fully than most men, realized his ambitions; he had been as successful as any of his contemporaries in the making of literature; he had won for himself through Euphemia, her husband, Pomona and Jonas, the Griffin and the Minor Canon, the transferred ghost, Mrs. Lecks and Mrs. Aleshine, and so many others, a host of admirers and affectionate enthusiasts. He makes friends still, for these people of his are very real, very dear, and, as Stockton intended them to be, at home in any company. Their warmth and their kindness and their memorable lives will not ever fade as long as there is an American literature.

Stockton did not quite finish the narrative links connecting the various disassociated stories in *John Gayther's Garden*. His wife, Marian Stockton, who had helped him for so long, in so many ways, finished it. The last word is hers:

The stories are all told. The winter has come. The Orchard is stripped of its leaves, and, sere and brown, they cover the garden paths and are strewn over the box borders. The fruits are all garnered. The bare vines that cover the summer-house are like dead memories of what has been. The vegetable-beds are empty. The black frost has settled upon bloom and foliage on the upper terrace. The sweet, blithe song of the red thrush has ceased. The family have gone to a sunnier clime. And John Gayther walks alone in his garden.

Chapter VIII

ANY just estimate of the contribution of Frank R. Stockton to American literature must inevitably place him in the second rank of those who were carrying the standard of American literary achievement during the last quarter of the nineteenth century. Led by the artistry and the philosophy of William Dean Howells (1837–1920), who exercised a double influence through his realistic novels and his urbane critical papers in *The Atlantic Monthly* and later in *Harper's Magazine*, the period during which Stockton was quietly dictating his best stories was one of intensive literary activity. Mark Twain (1835–1910) was a dominant figure whose *Tom Sawyer* had been published in 1876 while Stockton was still writing the *Rudder Grange* papers for *Scribner's Monthly*, and Twain's *Personal Recollections of Joan of Arc* (1895) coincided with one of Stockton's periods of greatest productivity. Henry James's (1843–1916) realistic studies of international contrasts, like *The Portrait of a Lady* (1881) and *The Tragic Muse* (1890), together with his great story of the supernatural, "The Turn of the Screw" (1898), were setting a standard of artistic achievement which has not since been equaled, except by Edith Wharton. Bret Harte (1836–1902), most artistic representative of the story of moral contrast, was exerting a marked influence on younger writers through the years that Stockton was quietly adding to his own reputation. These were the giants of those days, and the front-rank quality of their work is unquestionable.

Closely following such men as Howells, James, Twain, and Harte in artistry, however, came a little body of writers whose inspiration was not as great, whose influence was not as pronounced, but who were, nevertheless, writing ably and well.

It is with this group that Stockton belongs. Thomas Bailey Aldrich (1836–1907), nearest to Stockton in quality, was creating the gracious fantasy of "Marjorie Daw" (1873) while Harriet Prescott Spofford (1835–1920) had already, in "The Amber Gods" (1860), established for the romantic fantasy a nearly unapproachable standard. In romance, too, Dr. S. Weir Mitchell (1829–1914) was finding relaxation from his clinical practice, and Edward Eggleston (1837–1902) was still enjoying the curious success of *The Hoosier Schoolmaster* (1871), and writing such stories as *Roxy* (1878) and *The Faith Doctor* (1891). George W. Cable (1844–1925) was utilizing the wealth of material afforded by Creole life in Louisiana, and Francis Marion Crawford (1854–1909) was producing his discerning novels of Italian life. These were the contemporaries and the peers of Frank Stockton, and while each in his own way as an artist was necessarily something of an individualist, none was more individual, none was more free from the crowding literary influences of a brilliant period than Stockton.

Early in his writing career, Stockton had perceived clearly what he wished to do, and it would seem, too, that he had rather shrewdly judged his own limitations. Within those limitations he worked with admirable industry and a quiet joy, writing story after story without many of which American literature would be the poorer. Stockton's work reveals clearly how little he was influenced by the literary trends of his times. He was an individualist, indifferent to literary movements, indifferent to geography when the local-colorists were hymning of their own parishes, a practitioner of his craft with the matter-of-factness of the accomplished artificer. He was never a "literary" writer, and although many of his stories—*The Casting Away of Mrs. Lecks and Mrs. Aleshine, Rudder Grange,* "The Griffin and the Minor Canon," "The Lady, or the Tiger?", to mention but a few—are permanent additions to American literature, Stockton never persuaded himself that he was creating immortal fiction. He was a professional story-teller, interested in the life about him with the interest of the journalist, the editor, the author, who knows the requirements and the impermanence of the popular magazine. Unlike many of his contemporaries, William Dean Howells, James Lane Allen, Thomas Bailey Aldrich, for example, Stockton was not, in any scholarly sense, deeply read in the stream of English literature, although he did at times express his pleasure in Defoe and Dickens. In part this was due to defective sight, in greater part to the simple fact that he was not interested. On the few occasions when he discussed things literary, he wrote not as the critic, but as one activated by a personal and subjective purpose which concerned itself not at all with what other men had written. His scant half-dozen essays serve to illuminate his own work, express his working definitions of the essential difference between realism or romanticism, or his own methods of working up his stories.

Although he was born in Philadelphia, and lived there until his marriage, Stockton's tastes were for rural life and for the country scene. Seldom did he lay the entire scene of a story in the city, although this represented no revolt against urban life, nor did it reflect any adherence to the provincial movement. It was, rather, that he felt he could do more with his characters in the country. His urban characters are never as convincing as his country people, just as his fairies and his ghosts are more real, and more sympathetic, than his young men in love. A curious, but in an artist by no means unusual, quality existed in Stockton. Reality, for him, was meaningless unless it was webbed with fancy, but there was nothing of the impractical about his attitude toward his work. He asked for, and received, good prices from editors for his stories, and he utilized his time and his material with scrupulous thoroughness and economy. He sought no publicity, and rather shunned public references to his private life, except in such published interviews as any successful writer must submit to. Yet he has clearly set down in his stories more details of his life and travels than most men include in their formal biographies. Boyhood pranks, school experiences, love, marriage, house-hunting, the servant problem, travel, and the casual observations of day-by-day are all utilized effectively. He realized clearly the fact that anything in life, however incidental, is interesting if it is interestingly presented. Through the apparently simple process of vitalizing the commonplace by an ingenious overlay of the uncommon, Stockton produced story after successful story, when lesser writers would long since have been written out.

Stockton looked upon life with a passive but receptive interest. A clear thinker, but never a deep one, he was neither a philosopher seeking first causes, nor a cynic happily pointing out life's limitations. The human relationships he depicted in his stories are often superficial, but his attitude is always warmly sympathetic. He is writing at his best when he portrays homely, rural people who meet extraordinary circumstances, as do Mrs. Lecks and Mrs. Aleshine, or the Minor Canon, or Euphemia's husband (nameless hero!), with unamazed practicality. He is writing at his best when he is serenely contemplating the eminent *rightness* of disordered natural laws, like "Negative Gravity" or the doleful plight of "The Transferred Ghost."

The interest in Stockton's stories arises chiefly from character and situation, hardly ever from plot. While his short stories usually come to a neatly rounded point, his novels, from the standpoint of structure, consist chiefly of a series of connected episodes. But again generalization is dangerous, for in a type of fiction in which one would expect Stockton to be least successful, he produced, in *Kate Bonnet*, at least one well-articulated plot.

The style of Stockton's writing, because of its studied simplicity, is frequently overlooked by commentators on his work. Stockton is a stylist in a very real sense, even though his style belongs to an older and perhaps mellower tradition than that which has grown progressively less intelligible during the three decades since his death. His method is to strip his writing of all ornament, deliberately to remove any "literary" quality. The result is that he achieves his effects quickly, but with no appearance of haste—with, rather, a definite sense of leisure. His tones are chatty, informal, and he has that precision of phrase which adroitly conceals its own art. It seems, indeed, to be a style in keeping with the quill pens with which he wrote, suited to the easy pace of his stories, urbane and restrained. His diction follows definite patterns, but he has fewer irritating mannerisms than most authors who have written as voluminously. If he has not given us memorable phrases, it is because his diction is an instrument, and not an effect. It is the medium through which he produced his memorable pictures, the deft method whereby he created memorable people.

Frank R. Stockton's life was the life of a good man, and, for many reasons, one unmarked by great physical activity. One will find no purple patches in his story. But one will find in his life and in his work great dignity, industry, humor, and artistry. The world he has given us is a pleasant world into which we can escape, and from which we can return strengthened and refreshed, with our belief in the essential dignity of man restored to us. Not many writers can claim so much.

Bibliography

NOVELS AND COLLECTIONS

Ting-a-ling, Boston (Hurd and Houghton), 1870.
The Home—Where It Should Be and What to Put in It, N.Y.
   (G. P. Putnam), 1872. (With Marian E. Stockton.)
Roundabout Rambles in Lands of Fact and Fancy, N.Y. (Scribners), 1872.
What Might Have Been Expected, N.Y. (Dodd, Mead), 1874, 1898.
Tales Out of School, N.Y. (Scribner, Armstrong), 1875.
Rudder Grange, N.Y. (Scribners), 1879.
A Jolly Fellowship, N.Y. (Scribners), 1880.
The Floating Prince and Other Fairy Tales, N.Y. (Scribners), 1881.
   Contains: The Floating Prince
              How the Aristocrats Sailed Away
              The Reformed Pirate
              Huckleberry
              The Gudra's Daughter
              The Emergency Mistress
              A Sprig of Holly
              The Magician's Daughter and the High Born Boy
              Derido, or The Giant's Quilt
              The Castle of Bim
Ting-a-ling Tales, N.Y. (Scribners), 1882.
The Lady or the Tiger and Other Stories, N.Y. (Scribners), 1884,
   1886, 1891, 1893, 1900, 1907.
The Transferred Ghost, N.Y. (Scribners), 1884.
The Story of Viteau, N.Y. (Scribners), 1884.
A Christmas Wreck and Other Stories, N.Y. (Scribners), 1886.
   Contains: A Christmas Wreck
              A Story of Assisted Fate
              The Unhistoric Page
              A Tale of Negative Gravity

  The Cloverfield's Carriage
  The Remarkable Wreck of the "Thomas Hyke'
  My Bull-Calf
  The Discourager of Hesitancy
  A Borrowed Month
Stockton's Stories, First and Second Series, N.Y. (Scribners), 1886.
  First Series: *The Lady or the Tiger and Other Stories*
  Second Series: *The Christmas Wreck and Other Stories*
The Casting Away of Mrs. Lecks and Mrs. Aleshine, N.Y. (Century), 1886.
The Late Mrs. Null, N.Y. (Scribners), 1886, 1891, 1907.
The Bee-Man of Orn and Other Fanciful Tales, N.Y. (Scribners), 1887.
  Contains: The Bee-Man of Orn
             The Griffin and the Minor Canon
             Old Pipes and the Dryad
             The Queen's Museum
             Christmas Before Last
             Prince Hassak's March
             The Battle of the Third Cousins
             The Banished King
             The Philopena
The Hundredth Man, N.Y. (Century), 1887.
The Queen's Museum, N.Y. (Scribners), 1887, 1892, 1906.
  Contains: The Queen's Museum
             The Christmas Truants
             The Griffin and the Minor Canon
             Old Pipes and the Dryad
             The Bee-Man of Orn
             The Clocks of Rondaine
             Christmas Before Last
             Prince Hassak's March
             The Accommodating Circumstance
Amos Killbright: His Adscititious Experiences, with Other Stories, N.Y. (Scribners), 1888.
  Contains: Amos Killbright
             The Reversible Landscape
             Dusky Philosophy (I and II)
             Plain Fishing
The Dusantes, N.Y. (Century), 1888.

Personally Conducted, N.Y. (Scribners), 1889.

The Great War Syndicate, N.Y. (Collier), 1889; (Dodd, Mead), 1890.

Ardis Claverden, N.Y. (Dodd, Mead), 1890, 1894.

The Merry Chanter, N.Y. (Century), 1890.

The Stories of the Three Burglars, N.Y. (Dodd, Mead), 1890.

The House of Martha, Boston (Houghton Mifflin), 1891; N.Y. (Scribners), 1897.

The Rudder Grangers Abroad, N.Y. (Scribners), 1891.
  Contains: Euphemia Among the Pelicans
             The Rudder Grangers in England
             Pomona's Daughter
             Derelict
             The Baker of Barnbury
             The Water-Devil

The Squirrel Inn, N.Y. (Century), 1891, 1897.

The Clocks of Rondaine and Other Stories, N.Y. (Scribners), 1892.
  Contains: The Clocks of Rondaine
             The Curious History of a Message
             A Fortunate Opening
             The Christmas Truants
             The Tricycle of the Future
             The Accommodating Circumstance
             The Great Show in Kobal-land

The Watchmaker's Wife and Other Stories, N.Y. (Scribners), 1893.
  Contains: The Watchmaker's Wife
             Asaph
             My Terminal Moraine
             The Philosophy of Relative Existences
             The Knife That Killed Po Hancy
             The Christmas Shadrach
             The Reverend Ezekiel Crump

Pomona's Travels, N.Y. (Scribners), 1894.

Fanciful Tales, N.Y. (Scribners), 1894. Ed., Julia E. Langworthy.
  Contains: Old Pipes and the Dryad
             The Bee-Man of Orn
             The Clocks of Rondaine
             The Griffin and the Minor Canon
             The Christmas Truants

The Adventures of Captain Horn, N.Y. (Scribners), 1895, 1900, 1908.

A Chosen Few, N.Y. (Scribners), 1895.
  Contains: A Tale of Negative Gravity
           Asaph
           His Wife's Deceased Sister
           The Lady, or the Tiger?
           The Remarkable Wreck of the "Thomas Hyke"
           Old Pipes and the Dryad
           The Transferred Ghost
           A Philosophy of Relative Existences
           A Piece of Red Calico

Mrs. Cliff's Yacht, N.Y. (Scribners), 1896, 1900, 1907.

New Jersey, from the Discovery of the Scheyichbi to Recent Times, N.Y. (Appleton), 1896.

Stories of New Jersey, N.Y. (American Book Co.), 1896. (Reprint of *New Jersey, from the Discovery,* etc.)

Captain Chap, or The Rolling Stones, Phila. (Lippincott), 1897.

A Story-Teller's Pack, N.Y. (Scribners), 1897.
  Contains: The Magic Egg
           The Staying Power of Sir Rohan
           The Widow's Cruise
           Love Before Breakfast
           The Bishop's Ghost and the Printer's Baby
           Captain Eli's Best Ear
           As One Woman to Another
           My Well and What Came Out of It
           Stephen Skarridge's Christmas
           My Unwilling Neighbor

The Girl at Cobhurst, N.Y. (Scribners), 1898.

The Great Stone of Sardis, N.Y. (Harpers), 1898.

The Buccaneers and Pirates of Our Coast, N.Y. (Macmillan), 1898.

The Associate Hermits, N.Y. (Harpers), 1899.

The Vizier of the Two-Horned Alexander, N.Y. (Century), 1899.

The Young Master of Hyson Hall, Phila. (Lippincott), 1899.

The Novels and Stories of Frank R. Stockton, Shenandoah Edition, 23 vols., N.Y. 1899–1904.

Afield and Afloat, N.Y. (Scribners), 1900.
  Contains: The Buller-Podington Compact

A Romance of a Mule Car
The Governor-General
Old Applejoy's Ghost
Struck by a Boomerang
The Skipper and El Capitan
Come In, New Year!
A Sailor's Knot
The Great Staircase at Landover Hall
Ghosts in My Tower
A Landsman's Tale

A Bicycle of Cathay, N.Y. (Harpers), 1900.
Kate Bonnet, N.Y. (Appleton), 1902.
John Gayther's Garden, N.Y. (Scribners), 1902.
The Captain's Toll Gate, N.Y. (Appleton), 1903. (With Memoir and Bibliography by Marian E. Stockton.)
The Magic Egg and Other Stories, N.Y. (Scribners), 1907.
  Contains: The Magic Egg
             His Wife's Deceased Sister
             The Widow's Cruise
             Captain Eli's Best Ear
             Love Before Breakfast
             The Staying Power of Sir Rohan
             A Piece of Red Calico
             The Christmas Wreck
             My Well and What Came Out of It
             Mr. Tolman
             My Unwilling Neighbor
             Our Archery Club
Stories of the Spanish Main, N.Y. (Macmillan), 1913.
The Poor Count's Christmas, N.Y. (Stokes), 1927.

SHORT STORIES AND ARTICLES

N.B. Stockton's pseudonyms, *Paul Fort* and *John Lewees*, are indicated in parentheses. *Novels and Stories* refers to the Shenandoah Edition of the *Novels and Stories of Frank R. Stockton*, 23 vols., N.Y., 1899–1904.

About Otters (Lewees), *St. Nicholas*, Vol. IX (January 1882), p. 194.
Absent-Minded Botanist, The, in *Tales Out of School.*

(Retitled, "The Bee-Man of Orn")

Bee-Man of Orn, The

St. Nicholas, Vol. XI (November 1883), p. 46.

The Bee-Man of Orn (1887).

The Queen's Museum (1887).

Fanciful Tales (1894).

Beet Stretcher to the Head Binnick, The, *Hearth and Home,* Vol. III, September 16 & 23, 1871.

Bicycle of Cathay, A, *Harper's Magazine,* Vol. CI (June–October 1900), pp. 109, 177, 459, 619, 757.

Bishop's Ghost and the Printer's Baby, The

A Story-Teller's Pack, 1897.

Novels and Stories, Vol. XVII.

Blackgum ag'in' Thunder

Century, Vol. CXIII (December 1901), p. 248.

John Gayther's Garden (1902).

Novels and Stories, Vol. XXI.

Borrowed Month, A

Century, Vol. XXXI (February, March, 1886), pp. 537, 730.

A Christmas Wreck (1886).

The Lady or the Tiger? (1886).

Novels and Stories, Vol. XV.

Bottomless Black Pond (Lewees), *St. Nicholas,* Vol. VIII (May 1881), p. 502.

Boule de Neige de Leon Martin (Fort), *St. Nicholas,* Vol. I (January 1874), p. 151.

Boy's Own Phonograph, The (Lewees), *St. Nicholas,* Vol. VII (January 1880), p. 235.

Boy's Water Wheels, *Hearth and Home,* Vol. III, July 15, 1871.

Bron and Kruge, *Tales Out of School* (1875).

Buccaneers and Pirates of Our Coasts, The, *St. Nicholas,* Vol. XXV (November 1897–July 1898), pp. 4, 104, 212, 279, 386, 549, 652, 711.

Building of Rudder Grange, The, *The Youth's Companion,* Vol. LXVI (March 30, 1893), p. 161.

Buller-Podington Compact, The

Scribner's Monthly Magazine, Vol. XXII (August 1897), p. 217.

Afield and Afloat (1900).

Novels and Stories, Vol. XIV.

Bushwacker Nurse, The
   Cosmopolitan, Vol. XXVII (August 1899), p. 384.
   John Gayther's Garden (1902).
   Novels and Stories, Vol. XXI.
Camping Out at Rudder Grange, *Scribner's Magazine*, Vol. XVI
   (May 1878), p. 104.
Captain Eli's Best Ear
   Century, Vol. XXIX (December 1895), p. 227.
   A Story-Teller's Pack (1897).
   Novels and Stories, Vol. XVIII.
   The Magic Egg (1907).
Casting Away of Mrs. Lecks and Mrs. Aleshine, The, *Century*,
   Vol. X (August, September, October, 1886), pp. 595, 706, 870.
Castle of Bim, The
   St. Nicholas, Vol. VIII (October 1881), p. 899.
   The Floating Prince (1881).
Christmas Before Last, The
   St. Nicholas, Vol. XIII (December 1885), p. 124.
   The Bee-Man of Orn (1887).
   The Queen's Museum (1887).
   Novels and Stories, Vol. XVII.
Christmas Shadrach, The
   Century, Vol. XXI (December 1891), p. 177.
   The Watchmaker's Wife (1893).
   Novels and Stories, Vol. XVIII.
Christmas Truants, The
   The Queen's Museum (1887).
   The Clocks of Rondaine (1892).
   Fanciful Tales (1894).
Christmas Wreck, The
   The Christmas Wreck (1886).
   Novels and Stories, Vol. XVIII.
   The Magic Egg (1907).
   Great Modern American Stories, ed. W. D. Howells, 1920.
Cinderella, *St. Nicholas*, Vol. II (April 1875), p. 329.
Clocks of Rondaine, The
   St. Nicholas, Vol. XV (December 1887–January 1888), pp. 82,
   192.
   The Clocks of Rondaine (1892).
   The Queen's Museum (1892).

Fanciful Tales (1894).
Novels and Stories, Vol. XVII.

Cloverfield's Carriage, The
Century, Vol. IX (January 1886), p. 389.
A Christmas Wreck (1886).
Novels and Stories, Vol. XVI.

Colonel Myles' Adventures in Africa and India, *Tales Out of School.*

Come In, New Year!
Afield and Afloat (1900).
Novels and Stories, Vol. XIX.

Conscious Amanda, The
Cosmopolitan, Vol. XXIX (June 1900), p. 185.
John Gayther's Garden (1902).
Novels and Stories, Vol. XXI.

Cooking a Ghost, *Hearth and Home,* Vol. V, April 19, 1873.

Cot and the Rill, The
Cosmopolitan, Vol. XXVIII (December 1899), p. 209.
John Gayther's Garden (1902).
Novels and Stories, Vol. XXI.

Curious End of the General's Ride, The (Lewees), *St. Nicholas,*
Vol. IV (May, 1877), p. 434.

Curious History of a Message, The
St. Nicholas, Vol. XVI (December 1888), p. 84.
The Clocks of Rondaine (1892).

Deadly Sumach, The, *Hearth and Home,* Vol. II (September 24,
1870), p. 40.

Derelict
The Rudder Grangers Abroad (1891).
The Lady or the Tiger? (1891).
Novels and Stories, Vol. XV.

Derido, or, The Giant's Quilt, *The Floating Prince.*

Discourager of Hesitancy, The
Century, Vol. XXX (July 1885), p. 482.
The Lady or the Tiger? (1886).
A Christmas Wreck (1886).
Novels and Stories, Vol. XV.
Golden Book, Vol. IX (February 1929), p. 57.

Dogs of Noted Americans, *St. Nicholas,* Vol. XV (July 1888), p.
676.

Funny Darkies, *The Youth's Companion*, Vol. LXXI (November 11, 1897), p. 564.

Gentle Angler, The (Fort), *St. Nicholas*, Vol. I (September 1874), p. 627.

Ghosts in My Tower
Afield and Afloat (1900).
Novels and Stories, Vol. XIX.

Giant's Gift, The, *Hearth and Home*, Vol. II (January 1, 1870).

Gilded Idol and the King Conch Shell, The
John Gayther's Garden (1902).
Novels and Stories, Vol. XXI.

Girl at Rudder Grange, The
Scribner's Magazine, Vol. X (July 1875), p. 285.
Rudder Grange (1879).

Governor-General, The
Cosmopolitan, Vol. XXV (October 1898), p. 667.
Afield and Afloat (1900).
Novels and Stories, Vol. XIV.

Gandison's Quandary
Amos Killbright (1888).
Novels and Stories, Vol. VI.

Great Airline to the Moon, The, *Scribner's Magazine*, Vol. VII (December 1873), p. 260.

Great Show in Kobal-land, The, *The Clocks of Rondaine* (1892).

Great Staircase at Landover Hall, The, *Harper's Weekly*, Vol. XLII (December 17, 1898), p. 1233.

Great Stone of Sardis, The, *Harper's Monthly*, XCV (June–November 1897), pp. 19, 272, 380, 570, 736, 899.

Great Traveler, A (Lewees), *St. Nicholas*, Vol. II (February 1875), p. 254.

Great War Syndicate, The, *Collier's*, 1889.

Griffin and the Minor Canon, The
St. Nicholas, Vol. XII (October 1885), p. 896.
Fanciful Tales (1894).
The Bee-Man of Orn (1887).
Novels and Stories, Vol. XVII.
The Short Story, Boston, 1916, p. 210 (Ed., W. P. Atkinson).

Gudra's Daughter, The, *St. Nicholas*, Vol. VII (November 1879), p. 56.

Heni, *St. Nicholas*, Vol. IV (July 1877), p. 589.

In the Southeast Bastion, *Harper's Monthly,* Vol. LXIV (January 1882), p. 278.

Isle of June, An, *Scribner's Magazine,* Vol. XV (November 1877), p. 13.

Iturim and His Fortunes, *Tales Out of School* (1875).

John Gayther and the Galleon, *Cosmopolitan,* Vol. XXVII (June 1899), p. 183. (Appears also as "What I Found in the Sea.")

Johanna Sebus (Lewees), *St. Nicholas,* Vol. I (May 1874), p. 377.

Jolly Cabordmen, The, *Tales Out of School* (1875).

Jolly Fellowship, A, *St. Nicholas,* Vol. VI (November 1878–October 1879), pp. 13, 85, 210, 283, 349, 415, 480, 509, 572, 646, 749, 812.

Kate, *The Southern Literary Messenger,* New Series, Vol. VIII (December 1859), p. 415.

Kate Bonnet, *Collier's Weekly,* Vol. XXVI, 1902.

Knife That Killed Po Hancy, The
   The Great War Syndicate (1889).
   The Watchmaker's Wife (1893).
   Novels and Stories, Vol. VI.

Lady in the Box, The
   Cosmopolitan, Vol. XXVII (October 1899), p. 625.
   John Gayther's Garden (1902).
   Novels and Stories, Vol. XXI.

Lady, or the Tiger?, The
   Century, Vol. XXV (November 1882), p. 83.
   Kneass Philadelphia Magazine for the Blind, Vol. XXII, Philadelphia, 1888. (Braille).
   The Lady or the Tiger? (1884).
   A Chosen Few (1895).
   Novels and Stories, Vol. XV.
   Redpath's Library of Universal Literature, Vol. XXI.
   Century Magazine, Vol. LXXXV (February 1913), p. 534.
   A Book of Short Stories, Ed., S. P. Sherman, N.Y., 1914.
   Independent, Vol. XC (April 2, 1917), p. 28.
   Century Readings in the American Short Story, Ed., F. L. Pattee, N.Y., 1927, p. 260.
   Representative Modern Short Stories, Ed., A. Jessup, N.Y., 1929, p. 389.
   The Literature of America, Ed., A. H. Quinn, A. C. Baugh, W. D. Howe, N.Y., 1929, Vol. II, p. 950.

Molly's Sketch Book—and Mine, *St. Nicholas*, Vol. XLII (December 1914), p. 120.

Mother Pater's Pumpkin, *Hearth and Home*, Vol. I (November 27, 1869), p. 781.

Mrs. Cliff's Yacht, *Cosmopolitan*, Vol. XX (April 1896), p. 612.
   Vol. XXI (May–July 1896), pp. 45, 152, 304.

Mr. Tolman
   Harper's Monthly, Vol. LXI (August 1880), p. 371.
   The Lady or the Tiger? (1884).
   Novels and Stories, Vol. XVIII.
   The Magic Egg (1907).

Mumbo-Jumbo (Lewees), *St. Nicholas*, Vol. VIII (April 1881), p. 486.

My Balloon Hunt
   Ladies' Home Journal, Vol. XIX (March 1902), p. 56.
   John Gayther's Garden (1902).
   Novels and Stories, Vol. XXI.

My Brass Valise, *Putnam's*, Vol. XIII (June 1869), p. 679.

My Bull-Calf
   Harper's Monthly, LXIX (July 1884), p. 284.
   The Christmas Wreck (1886).
   Novels and Stories, Vol. XVI.

My Dogs, *The Youth's Companion*, Vol. LXXII (November 3, 1898), p. 547.

My Favorite Novelist and His Best Book
   Munsey's Magazine, Vol. XVII (June 1897), p. 351.
   Booklover, Vol. VIII (May–June 1901), p. 312.

Mysterious Barrel, The (Fort), *St. Nicholas*, Vol. IX (August 1882), p. 781.

Mystic Head-Waters, The, *Hearth and Home*, Vol. III (November 4, 1871).

My Terminal Moraine
   Once A Week, Vol. IX (April 26, 1892).
   The Watchmaker's Wife (1893).
   Novels and Stories, Vol. XV.

My Translataphone
   Harper's Bazaar, Vol. XXXIII (October 27–November 3, 1900), pp. 1612, 1678.
   John Gayther's Garden (1902).
   Novels and Stories, Vol. XXI.

My Unwilling Neighbor
  McClure's, Vol. VIII (December 1896), p. 155.
  A Story-Teller's Pack (1897).
  Novels and Stories, Vol. XVIII.
  The Magic Egg (1907).
My Well and What Came Out of It
  A Story-Teller's Pack (1897).
  Novels and Stories, Vol. XVIII.
  The Magic Egg (1907).
Naiad and the Dryad, The, *Hearth and Home,* Vol. II (August
  6, 1870), p. 33.
Nat Baker's Passenger, *The Youth's Companion,* Vol. LXXVII
  (January 8, 1903), p. 15.
New Rudder Grange, The, *Scribner's Magazine,* Vol. XV (Feb-
  ruary 1878), p. 532.
New Way to Go After Salt, A, *Riverside Magazine,* Vol. IV
  (April 1870), p. 179.
New Year's Call, A, *Hearth and Home,* Vol. V (January 4, 1873).
Northern Voice for the Dissolution of the Union, A (Privately
  printed), 1861.
Not So Stupid as He Seemed (Lewees), *St. Nicholas,* Vol. VIII
  (December 1880), p. 146.
Old Applejoy's Ghost
  Afield and Afloat (1900).
  Novels and Stories, Vol. XIX.
Old Nicolai (Fort), *St. Nicholas,* Vol. V (April 1878), p. 399.
Old Pipes and the Dryad
  St. Nicholas, Vol. XII (June 1885), p. 561.
  The Bee-Man of Orn (1887).
  The Queen's Museum (1887).
  Fanciful Tales (1894).
  A Chosen Few (1895).
  Novels and Stories, Vol. XVII.
One Tree Island, *St. Nicholas,* Vol. VII (July 1880), p. 722.
On the Refuge Sands, *St. Nicholas,* Vol. X (June 1883), p. 611.
On the Training of Parents
  Century, Vol. VI (May 1884), p. 123.
  The Lady or the Tiger? (1884).
On Wheels (Lewees), *St. Nicholas,* Vol. VI (September 1879), p.
  736.

Our Archery Club
  Scribner's Magazine, Vol. XVIII (August 1879), p. 542.
  The Lady or the Tiger? (1884).
  Novels and Stories, Vol. XVIII.
  The Magic Egg (1907).
Our Largest Friends (Lewees), *St. Nicholas,* Vol. IX (September 1879), p. 838.
Our Story
  Century, Vol. XXVI (September 1883), p. 762.
  The Lady or the Tiger? (1884).
  Novels and Stories, Vol. XV.
Our Tavern, *Scribner's Magazine,* Vol. XVI (August 1878), p. 470.
Out at Sea (Fort), *St. Nicholas,* Vol. VII (February 1880), p. 336.
Personally Conducted, *St. Nicholas,* Vol. XII (November–December 1884; February, August 1885), pp. 18, 127, 281, 733. Vol. XIII (November 1885; February, March, April, June 1886), pp. 38, 263, 349, 426, 572. Vol. XIV (June, July, October 1887), pp. 564, 648, 902. Vol. XV (March 1888), p. 347.
Peter's Rabbit Hunt (Fort), *St. Nicholas,* Vol. IV (September 1877), p. 752.
Philippine Embarrassment, A, *New York Sunday World,* November 12, 1899
Philopena, The
  St. Nicholas, Vol. XI (May 1884), p. 520.
  The Bee-Man of Orn (1887).
  The Queen's Museum (1887).
  Novels and Stories, Vol. XVII.
Philosophy of Relative Existences, A
  Century, Vol. XXII (August 1892), p. 536.
  The Watchmaker's Wife (1893).
  A Chosen Few (1895).
  Novels and Stories, Vol. XVII.
Piece of Red Calico, A
  The Lady or the Tiger? (1884).
  A Chosen Few (1895).
  Novels and Stories, Vol. XVIII.
  The Magic Egg (1907).
  The Golden Book, Vol. XIII (January 1931).

Pilgrim's Packets, The, *Scribner's Magazine,* Vol. V (January 1873), p. 333.
Plain Fishing
   Amos Killbright (1888).
   Novels and Stories, Vol. XVI.
Plums (Fort), *St. Nicholas,* Vol. VII (January 1880), p. 233.
Pomona and Jonas Tell a Story
   Century, LXI (November 1900), p. 120.
   John Gayther's Garden (1902).
   Novels and Stories, Vol. XXI.
Pomona's Bridal Trip, *Scribner's Magazine,* Vol. XVII (March 1879), p. 692.
Pomona's Daughter
   Century, XXVI (May 1883), p. 20.
   Rudder Grangers Abroad (1891).
   Novels and Stories, Vol. VIII.
Pomona Takes the Helm at Rudder Grange, *Scribner's Magazine,* Vol. XVI (July 1878), p. 407.
Poor Count's Christmas, The, *St. Nicholas,* Vol. IX (December 1881, January 1882), pp. 122, 189.
Poor Relations (Fort), *St. Nicholas,* Vol. VI (November 1878), p. 34.
Prince Hassak's March
   St. Nicholas, Vol. XI (December 1883), p. 141.
   The Bee-Man of Orn (1887).
   The Queen's Museum (1887).
   Novels and Stories, Vol. XVII.
Queen's Museum, The
   St. Nicholas, Vol. XI (September 1884), p. 837.
   The Bee-Man of Orn (1887).
   The Queen's Museum (1887).
   Novels and Stories, Vol. XVII.
Reformed Pirate, The, *The Floating Prince.*
Reformed Rats, The, *Hearth and Home,* Vol. I (January 30, 1869), p. 96.
Remarkable Wreck of the "Thomas Hyke," The
   Century, Vol. XXVIII (August 1884), p. 587.
   The Christmas Wreck (1886).
   A Chosen Few (1895).
   Novels and Stories, Vol. XVI.

Reversible Landscape, The
  Century, Vol. XXVIII (July 1884), p. 434.
  Amos Killbright (1888).
Reverend Ezekiel Crump, The, *The Watchmaker's Wife* (1893).
Romance of a Mule-Car, A
  Century, XXXIII (November 1897), p. 127.
  Afield and Afloat (1900).
  Novels and Stories, Vol. XIX.
Rudder Grange, *Scribner's Magazine*, Vol. IX (November 1874),
  p. 73.
Rudder Grangers in England
  Century, Vol. XXV (January 1883), p. 404.
  Rudder Grangers Abroad (1891).
  Novels and Stories, Vol. VIII.
Sailor's Knot, A
  Afield and Afloat (1900).
  Novels and Stories, Vol. XIX.
Sam Clemson the Second, *St. Nicholas*, Vol. IV (April 1877), p.
  361.
Sisters Three and the Kilmaree, *St. Nicholas*, Vol. IX (October
  1882), p. 942.
Skipper and El Capitan, The
  Cosmopolitan, Vol. XXVI (November 1898), p. 84.
  Afield and Afloat (1900).
  Novels and Stories, Vol. XIX.
Sleeping Courier, The, *St. Nicholas*, Vol. IV (May 1877), p. 426.
Slight Mistake, The, McMakin's *American Courier*, Philadelphia,
  September 1, 1855.
Snowflake of the Service, The
  Leslie's (October 1899).
  Strand (London), Vol. XVIII (October 1899), p. 401.
Snow-King, The, *St. Nicholas*, Vol. II (March 1875), p. 304.
Snow-Storm in the Tropics, A, *Tales Out of School* (1875).
Some Balloon Experiences (Lewees), *St. Nicholas*, Vol. IX (No-
  vember 1881), p. 30.
Something in the Old Clothes Line (Fort), *St. Nicholas*, Vol. V
  (January 1878), p. 211.
Spectral Mortgage, The
  Century, Vol. XXV (February 1883), p. 553.
  The Lady or the Tiger? (1884).

Novels and Stories, Vol. XI.

Story of Viteau, The, *St. Nicholas,* Vol. X (November 1882–April 1883), pp. 1, 84, 212, 284, 371, 412.

Story-Spoiler, The, *Independent,* Vol. LII (May 17, 1900), p. 1168.

Struck by a Boomerang
   Afield and Afloat (1900).
   Novels and Stories, Vol. XIX.

Sweet Marjorum Day, *St. Nicholas,* Vol. V (December 1877), p. 111.

Swords (Lewees), *St. Nicholas,* Vol. IX (July 1882), p. 701.

Tag's 'Coon, *St. Nicholas,* Vol. IX (July 1882), p. 683.

Tale of a Trap, The, *Hearth and Home,* Vol. III (September 9, 1871).

Tale of Negative Gravity, A, *Century,* XXIX (November 1884), p. 135.

Tender Heart, The, *Hearth and Home,* Vol. III (February 18, 1871), p. 133.

That Same Old Coon
   Scribner's Magazine, Vol. XVI (June 1878), p. 213
   The Lady or the Tiger? (1884).
   Novels and Stories, Vol. XV.

Ting-a-ling, *Riverside,* Vol. I (November, December 1867), pp. 512, 556.

Ting-a-ling and the Five Magicians, *Riverside,* Vol. III (February 1869), p. 57.

Ting-a-ling's Visit to Turilira, *Riverside,* Vol. III (July 1869), p. 317.

Tommy Hopper's Choice (Fort), *St. Nicholas,* Vol. I (November 1873), p. 4.

Tom Reynolds and Mariyama, *Tales Out of School* (1875).

Transferred Ghost, The
   Century, Vol. XXIV (May 1882), p. 43.
   The Lady or the Tiger? (1884).
   A Chosen Few (1895).
   Novels and Stories, Vol.`XV.
   Representative American Short Stories, Ed., W. T. Jessup.
   American Ghost Stories, Ed., C. A. Harper, Boston and N.Y., 1928.

Tricycle of the Future, The
   St. Nicholas, Vol. XII (May 1885), p. 481.

The Clocks of Rondaine (1892).

Trip to Blodgett's Island, A, *Hearth and Home,* Vol. III, (October 12, 1872).

Trouble She Caused When She Kissed, The, *Ladies' Home Journal,* Vol. XXVIII (December 1911), p. 17. (Retitle of "The Lost Dryad")

Truant Giants, The, *Hearth and Home,* Vol. I (December 11, 1869), p. 51.

Tweet, the Hermit Prince, *Hearth and Home,* Vol. I (August 14, 1869), p. 543.

Two Friends (Fort), *St. Nicholas,* Vol. II (March 1875), p. 265.

Unhistoric Page, An
   The Youth's Companion, Vol. LVIII (June 25, 1885) p. 249.
   A Christmas Wreck (1886).
   Novels and Stories, Vol. XVI.

Up a Tree, *Hearth and Home,* Vol. II (February 12, 1870).

Verney Ancestor (Fort), *St. Nicholas,* Vol. IX (November 1881), p. 38.

Vice-Consort, The, *Scribner's Magazine,* Vol. XXVIII (December 1900), p. 642.

Village of Wild Beasts, A, *St. Nicholas,* Vol. IV (August 1877), p. 651.

Vizier of the Two-Horned Alexander, The, *Century,* Vol. XXXV (November–December, 1898), pp. 52, 179.
   Vol. XXVI (January 1899), pp. 10, 746.

Voyage to the Lower Amazon, A, *Tales Out of School* (1875).

Watchmaker's Wife, The
   National Review (London), Vol. XXI, p. 240.
   The Watchmaker's Wife (1893).
   The Lady or the Tiger? (1884).

Water-Devil, The
   Scribner's Magazine, Vol. IX (October 1874), p. 108.
   Rudder Grangers Abroad (1891).
   Novels and Stories, Vol. XI.

What a Giant Found in the Sea, *Hearth and Home,* Vol. I (August 21, 1869), p. 35.

What I Found in the Sea
   Cosmopolitan, Vol. XXVII (June 1899), p. 183. (Under the title "John Gayther and the Galleon.")
   John Gayther's Garden (1902).

Novels and Stories, Vol. XXI.

What Might Have Been Expected, *St. Nicholas,* Vol. I (November 1873–October 1874), pp. 24, 88, 112, 222, 244, 362, 380, 487, 522, 611, 634, 733.

What They Did on Blodgett's Island, *Hearth and Home,* Vol. IV (October 19, 1872).

What Would You Have Done?, *The Youth's Companion,* Vol. LXXV (November 2, 1901), p. 613.

Widow's Cruise, The
   A Story-Teller's Pack (1897).
   Novels and Stories, Vol. XVIII.
   The Magic Egg (1907).
   Among the Humorists and After-Dinner Speakers, Ed. William Patten, Vol. III, N.Y., 1909.
   World's One Hundred Best Short Stories, Ed. Grant Overton, Vol. X.
   The Golden Book, Vol. XIII (June 1931), p. 56.

With Hook and Line, *The Youth's Companion,* Vol. LXXVI (June 12, 1902), p. 299.

Wolf and the Wheelbarrow, The, *The Youth's Companion,* January 1899.

Wonderful Ash Tree, The, *Tales Out of School* (1875).

Wonderful River, A (Fort), *St. Nicholas,* Vol. I (December 1873), p. 99.

Wonderful Tales of Gutefundus, *Tales Out of School* (1875).

Wrong Bird Story, The (Fort), *St. Nicholas,* Vol. I (April 1874), p. 344.

Selective Bibliography

BIOGRAPHICAL AND CRITICAL

Brown, T. Allston, *A History of the New York Stage.* From the First Performance in 1732 to 1901, N.Y., 1903 (Vol. III).

Chislett, William, Jr., *Moderns and Near Moderns,* N.Y., 1928.

Edmonds, Franklin Spencer, *The History of the Central High School of Philadelphia,* Phila., 1902.

Ellsworth, William W., *A Golden Age of Authors,* Boston and New York, 1919.

Firkins, Ina Ten Eyck, *Index to Short Stories,* N.Y., 1923.

Harkins, Edward F, *Little Pilgrimages Among Men Who Have Written Famous Books,* Boston, 1901.

Johnson, Merle, *American First Editions,* N.Y., 1932.

Johnson, Robert Underwood, *Remembered Yesterdays,* Boston, 1923.

Oberholtzer, Ellis Paxon, *A Literary History of Philadelphia,* Phila., 1906.

Pattee, Frank L., *A History of American Literature Since 1870,* N.Y., 1915.

Pattee, Frank L., *Development of the American Short Story,* N.Y., 1923.

Pforzheimer, Walter L., *Stocktoniana,* N.Y., 1936.

Phelps, William Lyon, *The Advance of the English Novel,* N.Y., 1916.

Quinn, Arthur Hobson, *American Fiction: An Historical and Critical Survey,* N.Y., 1936.

Stockton, Marian E., *Memoir of Frank R. Stockton, with a Bibliographical List of His Writings,* in *The Captain's Toll Gate,* Volume XXIII, Shenandoah Edition, *The Novels and Stories of Frank R. Stockton,* N.Y., 1899–1904.

Van Doren, Carl, *The American Novel,* N.Y., 1921.

Van Doren, Carl, *Frank R. Stockton,* in *The Dictionary of American Biography,* Vol. XVIII, pp. 42–44, N.Y., 1936.

Werner, William L., *The Escapes of Frank Stockton,* in *Essays in Honor of A. Howry Espenshade,* N.Y., 1937, pp. 21–45.

Vedder, Henry C., *American Writers of Today,* Boston, 1894.

PERIODICALS

"Frank R. Stockton" in *St. Nicholas Magazine,* VI (November 1878), pp. 46–47.

"Francis Richard Stockton: A Sketch," *Book Buyer,* II (December 1885), pp. 290–293.

"The Author of 'The Lady or the Tiger?'," C. C. Buel, *Century,* X (July 1886), p. 405.

"Stockton's Stories," William Dean Howells, *Atlantic Monthly,* LIX (January 1887), p. 130.

"Frank R. Stockton at Home," Julius Chambers, *Author,* III (July 15, 1891), p. 100.

"Frank R. Stockton," Edith M. Thomas, *McClure's Magazine,* I (November 1893), p. 467.

"An American Novelist," in "In the Public Eye," *Munsey's Magazine*, XVII (June 1897), p. 441.

"Stockton and His Works," William Dean Howells, *Harper's Weekly*, XLI (May 29, 1897), p. 538.

"Stockton at Home," J. H. Morse, *Critic*, XXXII (April 16, 1898), p. 259.

"Frank R. Stockton: Where He Wrote His Stories," T. F. Wolfe, *Lippincott's Magazine*, LXIV (September 1899), p. 367.

"Frank Stockton's New Home in West Virginia," C. Howard, *Ladies' Home Journal*, XVII (February 1900), p. 11.

"The Novels and Stories of Frank R. Stockton," William Dean Howells, *Book Buyer*, XX (February 1900), p. 19.

"Stockton and His Work," in "Fiction, New and Old," William Dean Howells, *Atlantic Monthly*, LXXXVII (January 1901).

"Francis Richard Stockton," *Harper's Weekly*, XLVI (May 3, 1902).

"Frank R. Stockton," Hamilton W. Mabie, *Book Buyer*, XXIV (June 1902), pp. 355–57.

"Stockton Pass-It-On Society," J. D. Bartley, *Book Buyer*, XXIV (July 1902), pp. 438–40.

"Frank R. Stockton," Edwin W. Bowen, *Sewanee Review*, XI (October 1903), p. 474.

"Stockton and His Girl Friend," Sara King Wiley, *Ladies' Home Journal*, XXIV (April 1907), p. 38.

"Frank R. Stockton," Edwin W. Bowen, *Sewanee Review* (July–September 1920).

"Pseudonyms and Sobriquets," Anne R. Marble, *Bookman*, LXXI (March 1930), p. 58.

"The Lady, the Tiger, and the Author," Walter L. Pforzheimer, *Colophon*, New Series, I, pp. 261–70.

PORTRAITS (selected)

Munsey's Magazine, XXV (July 1901), p. 487.
Century Magazine, LXIII (November 1901), p. 61.
Current Literature, XXXII (April 1902), p. 385.
Literary Digest, LIII (August 5, 1916), p. 305.

Index